Sport Management

Successful Private Sector
Business Strategies

Sport Management

Successful Private Sector Business Strategies

Kathleen A. Davis
Barry University

WCB Brown &
Benchmark
PUBLISHERS
Madison, Wisconsin • Dubuque, Iowa

Book Team

Executive Editor *Ed Bartell*
Editor *Scott Spoolman*
Developmental Editor *Susie Butler*
Production Editor *Karen A. Pluemer*
Art Editor / Processor *Kathleen Huinker Timp*
Permissions Coordinator *LouAnn Wilson*
Visuals / Design Developmental Consultant *Marilyn A. Phelps*
Visuals / Design Freelance Specialist *Mary L. Christianson*
Marketing Manager *Pamela S. Cooper*

A Division of Wm. C. Brown Communications, Inc.

Executive Vice President / General Manager *Thomas E. Doran*
Vice President / Editor in Chief *Edgar J. Laube*
Vice President / Sales and Marketing *Eric Ziegler*
Director of Production *Vickie Putman Caughron*
Director of Custom and Electronic Publishing *Chris Rogers*

Wm. C. Brown Communications, Inc.

President and Chief Executive Officer *G. Franklin Lewis*
Corporate Senior Vice President and Chief Financial Officer *Robert Chesterman*
Corporate Senior Vice President and President of Manufacturing *Roger Meyer*

The credits section for this book begins on page 289 and is
considered an extension of the copyright page.

Cover design by Fulton Design

Cover image by Don Landwehrle / The Image Bank

Copyedited by Linda L. Gomoll

A Times Mirror Company

Library of Congress Catalog Card Number: 93-70907

ISBN 0-697-13995-6

Printed in the United States of America by Wm. C. Brown Communications, Inc.,
2460 Kerper Boulevard, Dubuque, IA 52001

10 9 8 7 6 5 4 3 2 1

*To my parents, Bill and Dolores, who taught me to play hard,
strive for excellence, and never look back.*

BRIEF CONTENTS

EXPANDED CONTENTS

PART II: THE SPORT MANAGER'S WORK

PART III: MANAGING PEOPLE

PART IV: SPECIAL TOPICS IN SPORT MANAGEMENT

PART V: THE SHAPE OF THE INDUSTRY

PREFACE

This book was develped to educate present and future sport managers about the skills and competencies required to successfully manage in the sport management private sector. Currently, very few textbooks utilize general management theory and principles making direct application to the sport management field. Additionally, no textbook to date addresses the three broad private sector sport management segments—consumer, spectator, and participant. Finally, using the case study approach, this textbook integrates theory with practical application throughout each chapter of the book. These various facets of the book create a unique and effective means of educating those pursuing sport management careers about the finer points of managing private sector sport businesses.

The textbook primarily targets entry-level undergraduate students in sport management. A secondary market for the text would be the practicing sport managers who simply want to polish their management skills and techniques. With limited textbook resources available to those pursuing sport management careers, this textbook adds to and complements the existing body of knowledge in sport management.

Arranged in a straightforward fashion, the book introduces students initially to the exciting opportunities in private sector sport management. Then it explores the management competencies required to operate a successful sport business. The third section of the book introduces the necessary "people" skills each sport manager should possess. The fourth and final sections of the textbook cover special topics and applications required of managers in the private sector.

The uniqueness in this textbook stems from its "user-friendly" approach. The simplified terms and phraseology, coupled with light and humorous quips at errant managers, provide readers with a refreshing style and approach to the study of sport management. Each chapter begins with a scenario of "what *not* to do" as an aspiring manager and then through the course of the chapter, remedies to the scenario are posited. This provides for a fun, problem-solving approach to the successful management of sport in the private sector.

Chapter summaries and review questions provide useful learning aides for the reader. These tools also help to link ideas and concepts together throughout the textbook to provide an integrative approach to learning. Many examples of real-world management experiences are incorporated into the text to further the learning applications of the reader. A special thanks for the hard work by the following reviewers, whose suggestions and comments helped to successfully package a more complete and meaningful product.

James D. LaPoint
University of Kansas

Mary Dale Blanton
University of Tennessee, Knoxville

James R. Ewers
University of Utah

Jan Boyungs
Central Washington University

Gary R. Gray
Iowa State University

Additionally, many thanks to Karen Pluemer, Linda Gomoll, and Susie Butler of Brown & Benchmark, whose editing and manuscript deliberations helped to bring this project to fruition.

Introduction

This introductory section welcomes you to the wonderful world of sport management. It will expose you to the fundamental elements of the field—sport management definitions, managing people and operations, and managing in the work environment. It will also provide you with successful strategies for professional preparation and career opportunities in the field. Let's get started!

*Home of the Class
AA Jacksonville
Suns, Wolfson Park is
part of the
Jacksonville sports
complex that also
includes the Gator
Bowl and Veterans
Memorial Coliseum.
Recently refurbished,
the facility has
seating for 7,200
patrons.*

Why Sport Management?

DEFINITION OF THE FIELD OF SPORT MANAGEMENT

Have you ever asked yourself these questions:

- Who is responsible for organizing the Boston Marathon?
- Who plans game day operations for the Yankees versus the Toronto Blue Jays?
- Who provides the comfortable workout environment at your local health spa?
- Who is responsible for product management at Titleist Golf Division?
- How do players like Dan Marino manage their careers?
- Where do those wonderful trip ideas from Club Med come from?
- Who makes it possible for us to enjoy watching a tennis match between Monica Seles and Steffi Graf?

If you answered sport managers, you are absolutely right! Sport managers are the wonderful glue that binds successful sport organizations, sport events, athletes, health clubs, and virtually every sport industry-related business. Think about it for a moment. We enjoy the high-energy level at a professional football game; we work out in Reebok cross trainers; we recreate at the worksite employee fitness facility—all made possible by the organized efforts of sport managers. These managers make the decisions that affect the future direction of sports in our society.

Not only is it important that you understand the impact sport has on our lives and the direct influence sport managers have on the virtual existence of sports, but it is relevant that you understand the field of sport management and how it influences you. If you desire to become a sport manager, this book will provide you with the tools to successfully manage in the sport management industry. If you plan to work in the industry and not manage, this book will give you valuable insight into how sport managers operate and function, and strengthen your working relationship with them. Finally, even if you've recently won the lottery and will never work the rest of your life, the information this book provides will help to explain why and how managers make decisions. Table 1.1 provides examples of sport organizations that require sport managers.

TABLE 1.1 Sport Organizations Requiring Sport Managers	
Industry Segment	**Example**
Service Industries	Health Clubs, Resorts, Tourism, Corporate Fitness, Professional Sports
Health-related Industries	Wellness Programs Sport Medicine Clinics Cardiac Rehabilitation Clinics
Sporting Goods Manufacturing	Reebok, Nike, Foot-Joy, Nautilus, Converse, Spaulding, other
Sport Management Specialization Areas	Sport Marketing Firms Sport Public Relations Firms Special Event Management Sport Agents Sport Consulting Firms

Who Are Sport Managers?

What does a sport manager do? Their jobs entail a variety of management functions performed in the uniqueness of each sport setting. They **plan, organize, control, lead, motivate, direct,** and make **decisions.** They perform these functions both internally, within the confines of the sport organization, and externally, impacting social and cultural forces in the environment.

This book will be devoted to the study of managing privately owned and operated sport businesses. These facilities will include health and fitness clubs, corporate fitness facilities, arena/dome facilities, and sporting goods manufacturers.

Public sport businesses will not be addressed in this text. These include sport programs such as secondary and collegiate athletic programs, amateur athletics, and state- or federally-sponsored athletic programs.

Why Study Sport Management?

Whether you plan to pursue careers in athletic training, exercise physiology, health promotion, or as a sport manager, it is vital that you become familiar with the field of sport management for several important reasons.

First, the impact sports has on society cannot be undervalued. According to recent fitness in America surveys, 97 percent of Americans believe that exercise is important to a healthy life-style, with over 50 percent of these individuals actually performing some kind of fitness activity on a regular basis (McCarthy, 1989). These results emphasize more than ever how sports and fitness activities impact the personal fitness life-styles of individuals.

A second reason for examining the field of sport management hinges on the decision-making influence sport managers have on the future direction of sport-related services and products. Sport managers have the power to allocate resources to a variety of sources. They are responsible for building safe batting machines, organizing successful road races, maintaining and promoting successful and profitable health clubs. Sport managers help to establish jobs, impact healthy life-styles, create new sport products and services, and organize sport events. It would be very challenging to find someone who is not influenced in some way by the work of sport managers.

Thirdly, it is interesting to see how many individuals who were not trained in sport management, often find themselves in some kind of management position. Many people who are trained in athletic training, exercise physiology, or physical education often work their way up the ladder in sport organizations and find themselves managing. They may find themselves in fitness director positions, directing health promotion programs, or chairing physical education departments at high schools or universities. Every organization must have managers to assure successful operation of that organization.

Finally, regardless of what position we hold in the sport industry, we are responsible to, directed by, and greatly influenced by those in managerial positions. Therefore, our ability to empathize with the day-to-day functions a sport manager performs will assist our own work performance as well as the manager's ability to function. If, for example, your manager requests a sport marketing budget from you, knowledge of budgeting and the control function of sport management will allow you to successfully compile a line item budget request, all made possible through the information received in later chapters of this text.

The following section will complete the chapter with a discussion about the broad task categories that sport managers, regardless of their position, perform. This will give the reader valuable insight into the rationale for organization of the book and what tasks they must master to become a proficient sport manager in the 1990s.

TABLE 1.2 Sport Management Industry Sectors

Consumer (Driven by purchase power)	Spectator (Driven by team support/affiliation)	Participant (Driven by a person's need to achieve or accomplish a goal)
Yankees (T-shirts, concessions, etc.) Nike Reebok New Balance Titleist	Yankees (Fans) Davis Cup Tennis Tournament Bob Hope Desert Classic	Yankees (Players) Boston Marathon Health Club/Spa/Resort Members

Sport Management Industry Segments

Any discussion of sport management must encompass a basic understanding of the field of *sport management*. The definition of sport management, first proposed by Sheffield and Davis in 1986, perhaps provides the most simplistic view of the field. Professionals in sport management perform their daily management tasks in either a consumer-oriented industry, a spectator-driven industry, or a participant-focused industry—the involved profit model (IPM). Some businesses are so broad and diverse that they operate in all three domains or sectors. Table 1.2 helps to better explain these sectors and IPM, and also provides you with some examples of sport businesses that operate in each.

As you can see, most sport businesses fall into three broad categories. For example, corporate fitness programs provide a more narrow business focus targeting only one segment, namely, employee participation. There are, however, exceptions to these divisions. For example, arena/dome management (i.e., Yankees) covers all three categories: they sell a commodity (concessions); they provide opportunities for participants (professional athletes); and they attract people to watch (spectators).

Additionally, table 1.2 helps to explain that sport managers are also responsible for understanding the needs and wants of their **clientele.** All people are driven by three basic motivators—the need to achieve, perform more capably, and affiliate with a favorite sport team (McClelland, 1975). Future sport managers must address these needs to successfully market their ideas, services, or products.

TASK SPECIFICITY AND THE SPORT MANAGER

Sport managers must be proficient in three broad task categories (Dubin, 1982):

> Managing the workplace
>
> Managing people
>
> Managing day-to-day operations

Regardless of the nature of the business, every sport manager must perform the tasks described above. Their responsibilities go beyond mere "trouble shooting," managing their own work environment and schedule, and strategically planning a sport business portfolio. Their work requires an in-depth understanding of *all* these roles and responsibilities. These tasks will provide a point of departure for travel into the study of sport management and a framework for the organization of this text.

Managing the Workplace

This task area refers to the management of individual sport organizations. The Boston Marathon requires a year-round planning cycle. Health clubs must organize the various departments and programs to assure efforts are coordinated effectively and efficiently. The sport manager at a sporting goods store must hire competent employees and monitor their performance levels. Membership numbers must be projected, new facilities planned, and business cycles and profits tracked. All of these special tasks involve effectively managing the work environment of sport businesses.

Managing People

Whether managing a professional team, a corporate fitness facility, or a local country club, you are only as good as the people who work for you. As easy as it sounds, the need to effectively manage people cannot be stressed enough. Motivated employees perform better—which translates into increased profits (Davis, 1988). Open lines of communication help to create an organization free of conflict and strife. Sport managers must also learn how to handle interpersonal relations among employees and lead them toward greater performance levels.

Managing Day-to-Day Operations

It is generally understood that every sport organization "does" something. They manufacture shoes, sponsor special events, market professional athletes, provide an optimal fitness environment for clientele, and provide a workout facility for the vacationing family or weary business traveler. Daily efforts of staff and management provide the "means" to these "ends." The following chapters will show how to best supervise these efforts.

Each task area discussed in the following chapters must be studied not only as mutually independent areas of study but also for their mutually dependent relationships, each relying on the successful operation of the others.

Let's venture into the wonderful world of sport management!

SUMMARY

1. The industry can be divided into three broad segments: consumer, spectator, and participant.
2. Each industry segment is driven by satisfying basic human needs and desires. Understanding the relationship of these segments when meeting basic human needs helps to assure a more profitable sport enterprise.
3. Sport managers plan, organize, and control events in a sport environment. To accomplish this they must have a working knowledge of managing day-to-day operations.
4. A knowledge of the field of sport management is important even if you don't plan to manage because it helps you understand the rationale behind managers' decisions.

REVIEW QUESTIONS

1. Who is responsible for creating a safe playing environment at a soccer match?
2. What is meant by privately owned and operated sport business? Cite examples.
3. What are the three industry segments that make up the sport management field?
4. What skills are essential when "managing people"?

How to Succeed as a Sport Manager
The Bottom Line—Professional Preparation

■ ■ ■ ■ ■ ■ ■

CASE STUDY
Welcome to the Wonderful World of Sport Management!

Bob Parrish graduated from State University with a B.S. in communications. His first job out of college was the public relations director for Better Bounce Shoes International where he was responsible for communicating with both internal and external publics associated with Better Bounce. He stayed in that position for approximately three years before being offered a job to become product manager of their tennis division.

This promotion will give Bob a significant raise and also carry with it valuable management experience—he will be primarily in charge of personnel and decisions associated with the sales and marketing of their tennis shoe products.

As Bob reviews the possibility of accepting the position, he remembers a course he took in sport management. This course really helped to stimulate Bob's interest in the sport management field as a possible career. His only hesitation in taking the position is accepting all the new responsibilities associated with the position. Also, he is concerned about how he will manage employees (many are close friends) who he has just worked with side-by-side. This is Bob's big opportunity to advance professionally. Who knows when the chance will come around again? He will be responsible for two secretaries, three salespersons, and four marketing representatives.

DISCUSSION QUESTIONS

1. *How will Bob's experience with Better Bounce make him a more effective manager?*
2. *Should Bob be concerned about managing his friends?*
3. *What other skills or abilities introduced in his sport management course can Bob apply to this new position?*

■ ■ ■ ■ ■ ■ ■

THE GROWTH OF EDUCATIONAL PROGRAMS

The past twenty-five years has seen significant developments in sport management career preparation. The first program initiated in this field was developed by a collaborated effort of Dr. James Mason of Ohio University and the late Walter O'Malley, owner of the Los Angeles Dodgers in 1967 (Mason, Higgins, & Williamson, 1981). Initially, programs of this nature offered courses only through physical education, leisure, and recreation departments. They also provided professional preparation solely within the physical education administration realm, often preparing people to become administrators of athletic, recreation, and physical education programs. As the field of sport management became more sophisticated, so too did the professional preparation of sport managers. Coursework *outside* of recreation and physical education programs became the rule rather than the exception. Students looked to business departments for additional exposure to knowledge about finance, accounting, organizational behavior, marketing, public relations and communications, for example. Curricula became more standardized and accrediting agencies such as AALR (American Association for Leisure and Recreation), NASSM (North American Society of Sport Management), and NASPE (National Association for Sport and Physical Education) helped establish guidelines for undergraduate and graduate preparation in the field.

Presently, most professional preparation programs attempt to include a general survey course in sport management opportunities, an internship or practicum course to help provide the "real world" practical experiences or field exposure, and several general business courses. This "core" of professional preparation helps to lay the foundational skills required of every manager, regardless of what job or segment they manage. Elective courses then typically allow students to specialize in an assorted career tract. For example, if one wanted to market the San Diego Padres baseball team, they would take additional coursework in marketing, public relations, and marketing management. Or if one wanted to manage a fitness program at a health spa, they would develop competencies in exercise physiology, exercise prescription, nutrition, or health promotion program planning. Further specialization can also be facilitated with the assistance of a properly chosen internship or practicum experience. This educational experience typically culminates a student's professional preparation experience with a university. Proper selection of an internship site is critical to gain a complete overview of the working environment a student might eventually manage. The internship, in many cases, leads to future employment with the host site or a job reference when the search for employment in the industry does begin. Internships typically involve, on the average, 300 contact hours with a host site and generally require a project summarizing internship activities or on-the-job projects completed.

CAREER OPPORTUNITIES

Once professional preparation has been completed, the job search begins. The sport management field provides many unique and exciting job opportunities for the future manager. Table 2.1 describes some general job categories and responsibilities available to interested students in the field of sport management. Table 2.2 addresses the average salary for positions in the industry (Rice, 1992). Most students are guided into these careers with the help of capable advisors, campus job placement offices, and/or internship supervisors. Be sure to exhaust all sources available when attempting your job search.

TABLE 2.1 Career Opportunities in Sport Management

Area	Responsibilities
Professional Sport:	
General Manager	Responsible for general program administration, personnel evaluation, labor relations, player talent evaluation
Director of Marketing	Selects and targets possible markets for ticket sales Develops corporate sponsorships Establishes promotional events and gimmicks Prepares marketing research reports
Director of Public Relations	Develops, implements, and maintains positive relations with the team and local community Establishes positive press relationships Assures effective communication between the team, management, and surrounding community
Ticket Manager	Keeps accurate ticket accounts for all the games Assures effective and efficient ticket sales at both the stadium and ticket sales outlets
Arena Facility Management:	
Facility Director	Responsible for media relations, labor relations, program planning, budget presentation, and management
Operations Manager	Responsible for event management, marketing, financial supervision, dealing with day-to-day operations
Box Office Manager	Coordinates all ticket operations and sales
Personnel Manager	Hires and trains all employees needed for facility operation
Stage Manager	Responsible for pre-event setup (includes lighting, stage setup, and sound system installation)

TABLE 2.1 *continued*

Area	Responsibilities
Concession Manager	Coordinates sales Processes orders Maintains concession areas and equipment Staffs and supervises employees to operate concession areas
Sport Club Management:	
General Manager	Responsible for hiring and supervising first-level management Develops and implements operating budget Responds to owners' needs and business goals Attracts and maintains membership base
Fitness Director	Responsible for fitness programming; membership services, assessment, and prescription; hiring and supervising fitness staff
Sales/Marketing Director	Seeks out new membership opportunities Promotes sales Supervises and trains sales staff
Racquet Sports Director	Develops and implements racquet sports programming Sets up tournament and special promotional events Trains and supervises racquet sports instructors
Aquatics Director	Teaches and/or coaches all levels of participants Conducts and promotes special aquatics events Schedules pool activities Oversees equipment and facility maintenance
Sport Entrepreneurs/Consultants:	
Entrepreneurs	Create a demand for a new product or service Control costs and budgets for product or service Procure investment capital and generate revenue
Consultants	Conduct market studies Assist companies in program development, facility design, and assessment Develop business plans and/or marketing strategies
Sport Product Management:	
President/CEO	Supervises company's productions and operations
Senior VP Operations	Directs plant operations
Senior VP Marketing	Directs communication strategies
VP Sales	Supervises sales strategies and sales representatives

As you can see from table 2.1, the field elicits a variety of employment opportunities. Table 2.2 gives entry-level, average, and top-level earning potential for various careers in sport management. With the assistance of a solid core of coursework, coupled with judicial selection of elective courses and an internship site, students can help to assure their future job successes in the industry. Part-time and seasonal work experiences also provide students with industry experience that will also increase their chances of employment. Table 2.3 provides some valuable guidelines for future sport managers to assist them in acquiring career opportunities in the industry.

TABLE 2.2 Sports Careers Salary Survey

Sport Careers	Intro.	Average	Top Level
Athlete Agent (Contracts)	10,000	50,000	1,000,000
Athlete Agent (Endorsements)	18,000	50,000	300,000
Manager of Amateur Association	12,000	25,000	50,000
Clubhouse Manager	Minimum	40,000	150,000
College Coach	20,000	35,000	1,000,000
Professional Coach	35,000	60,000	1,000,000
Strength & Conditioning Coach	25,000	40,000	110,000
College Athletic Director	45,000	70,000	200,000
Associate Athletic Director	30,000	45,000	75,000
Athletic Counseling	12,000	25,000	45,000
Enforcement/Compliance	20,000	35,000	70,000
Equipment Manager (College)	17,000	30,000	45,000
Facilities Management (College)	20,000	40,000	70,000
Fund Raising (College)	20,000	40,000	60,000
Marketing (College)	17,000	35,000	50,000
Sports Information Director	12,000	35,000	60,000
Tickets (College)	15,000	30,000	40,000
Women's Athletic Administrator	25,000	45,000	100,000
Corporate Sponsorships	12,000	40,000	125,000
Customer Relations	15,000	30,000	55,000
Sports Engineer	32,000	50,000	150,000
Equipment Manager	15,000	35,000	150,000
Facility Management	20,000	35,000	150,000
Financial Management	20,000	35,000	150,000
Sportswriter/Columnist	10,000	40,000	250,000
Editor	10,000	40,000	150,000

TABLE 2.2 *continued*

Sport Careers	Intro.	Average	Top Level
Luxury Box Sales/Management	18,000	30,000	60,000
Manufacturer's Representative	15,000	40,000	150,000
Market Researcher	15,000	35,000	80,000
Sports Marketing Director	18,000	35,000	250,000
Merchandising Manager	20,000	40,000	100,000
Human Relations Director	15,000	40,000	90,000
Promotional Item Manager	15,000	30,000	60,000
Promotions Director	25,000	40,000	80,000
Public Relations Manager	12,000	30,000	100,000
Broadcaster	15,000	30,000	500,000
Broadcast Producer	15,000	25,000	100,000
Sports Sales	12,000	35,000	250,000
Scouting	25,000	35,000	100,000
Special Events Manager	18,000	35,000	85,000
Television Associate Director	30,000	50,000	75,000
Television Associate Producer	25,000	40,000	60,000
Television Director	25,000	50,000	750,000

Reprinted with the permission of Collier Books, an imprint of Macmillan Publishing Company from *How To Get a Job in Sports: The Guide to Finding the Right Sports Career* by John Taylor. Copyright © 1992 by John Taylor.

TABLE 2.3 Checklist for Sport and Leisure Management Professionals*

Professional Preparation
Part 1: Education

1. Are you conversant in the professional vocabulary of sport and leisure management?

2. Can you evaluate computer software for its utility in SLEM environs?

3. Does your course of study include relevant coursework in business, leisure, physical education, psychology, sociology, management and recreation?

4. Do you have a good working knowledge of measurement and evaluation for personnel and professional accountability and advocacy?

5. Is there a coherent theme throughout your discretionary coursework?

6. Do you have "hard copy" of relevant coursework to use in a job interview?

7. Do you possess personal competence in one or more sport or leisure activity forms?

8. Do you possess instructional competence in one or more sport or leisure activity forms?

9. Do you possess current certification, licensure, credentials for number 8?

10. Do you have a good grasp of the mechanics of active listening?

11. Are you adept at written and oral communication? (KISS style)

TABLE 2.3 *continued*

Part 2: Job-Related Experience

12. Are your part-time/seasonal jobs providing relevant (job-related supervisory, budgetary) experience?
13. Can you document instances of your initiative (improvements, cost-savings, ideas) that increased productivity on the job?
14. Have you explored the feasibility of participating in your campus sponsored co-oping program?
15. For each of your most important job-related experiences, can you list:
    a. Five things you can do?
    b. Five things you learned?
    c. Several contributions you made or things you accomplished?

Job-Seeking Behaviors
Part 3: Networking

16. Can you name at least three fields of employment into which you might fit?
17. Can you name at least 10 kinds of employers that might hire a person with your background?
18. Do you know four or five resources to help you find answers to questions 16 and 17?
19. Can you name at least four sources of information that could help you discover potential employers in a particular geographical area?
20. In the past month, have you talked to at least three people who are employed in your field of interest with the purpose of learning more about what they do?

Part 4: Resumes and Interviewing

21. Do you have a resume with which you are satisfied?
22. Do you have functional and chronological resumes?
23. Have you asked employers for feedback on your resume?
24. When you apply to an employer, do you send your resume to the department head as well as the personnel office?
25. Are you familiar with the organizational structure, services/programs/products of the employers to whom you are applying?
26. Can you clearly state your career goals?
27. Can you explain why you chose your major?
28. Can you describe your greatest strength?
29. Can you describe your greatest weakness?
30. Can you name the work activities you do most well and most enjoy? How about non-work activities?
31. Can you list at least five job skills and abilities you have?
32. Can you clearly state why you are interested in working for each employer to whom you apply?
33. Have you used any of the following methods to prepare for an interview:
    a. Role playing with a friend or relative?
    b. Writing answers to common interview questions?
    c. Role playing in front of a mirror?
    d. Manuals and services offered by your placement office?
    e. Examined wardrobe in mirror?

Source: From "Job Search Strategies—Where in Your Job Search Are You?" from the Office of Career Planning and Placement, University of Tennessee, Knoxville, TN.

FUTURE DIRECTIONS OF THE FIELD

Or in other words, where do we go from here? The future does indeed look bright for business growth and career opportunities in sport management. Futurists, market analysts, opportunists all agree on one thing: the field will continue to grow and develop through the year 2000. What areas will see the most growth and promise? Let's gaze into the crystal ball and review possibilities in the three industry segments.

The Health and Fitness Industry

We will continue to see market specialization and tighter controls when managing these commercial enterprises. Growth in family markets will continue and "nitch" markets (for women only, fitness for the elderly, fitness programs for obese individuals) will thrive. With people incorporating fitness into a part of their life-style, spending and time devoted to these activities is becoming a necessity rather than a frill. Other positive growth indicators can be seen by the recent interest of large corporations (Bally and the Hilton hotels, for example) in developing or acquiring fitness facilities for clientele use (Deveroux, 1991).

Arena and Dome Management

Also experiencing moderate growth is the arena and dome management area. Since the early 1960s these sport facilities have grown in numbers with close to 2,000 sport arenas in cities and municipalities around the country. There has been ever-growing interest by private sector management groups which seek to manage and control these facilities. For this reason, a number of sport commissions have been developed by municipalities to assist both public and private business operation of these facilities. Figure 2.1 highlights sales increases from 1990 to 1991 in the sports equipment market.

Sporting Goods Management

As companies such as Reebok or Nike attempt to become more and more diversified in the type and variety of products they produce, so will the demand for trained personnel in these businesses. These companies look for specialized training and talent in their search for qualified employees. Sport

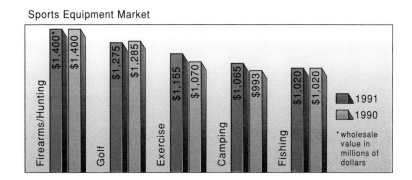

Sports Equipment Market

FIGURE 2.1
Sales grew by 2.2%
because of sales
strength of camping
and exercise
equipment.

management program graduates typically possess the qualifications and potential to fill these positions. Additionally, with product sales continuing to escalate, the future looks bright for employment in this area.

SUMMARY

1. Professional preparation should include coursework in both business and sport, and should culminate with an internship opportunity.
2. Career opportunities exist in a variety of settings. Selecting an appropriate internship and acquiring part-time work experiences help the future sport manager to be more competitive in the job marketplace.
3. A viable job candidate is one who is proficient in three areas of professional preparation. These areas include education, job-related experiences, and networking capabilities.

REVIEW QUESTIONS

1. What factors have contributed most to the development of professional preparation during the last 25 years? Why?
2. Why should an internship culminate a manager's educational experience?
3. Choose a career from table 2.1. Now list what appropriate electives one might take to assure proper professional preparation for the job.
4. List three reasons why job-related experiences are so important.

The Sport Manager's Work

This section addresses the rudimentary sports
management tasks of planning, organizing,
and controlling. These basic tasks comprise the
work performed regardless of the type or
nature of the business operated. Also covered
in this section is the decision-making process
and ways it affects how a manager plans,
organizes, and controls. Let's get back
to basics!

*Executive Suite lobby
area of Joe Robbie
Stadium.*

The World of the Sport Manager

■ ■ ■ ■ ■ ■ ■

CASE STUDY
There's Only ONE Best Way to Manage 'Round Here

George Ruggles came to the small town of Tumbleweed, Texas with plenty of job experience in managing corporate fitness programs. He had held a successful program director's position with Honnoco Oil in Dallas and was ready to move with his wife and two children from the big city environment to the rural, less hectic pace of country living. When George learned of the position at Tumbleweed, it was a dream come true. He would be managing a smaller scale corporate fitness program with Texas-T Oil Company. He would take the place of Tom Willis who was retiring from the position after fifteen years of faithful service. His responsibilities included managing the existing fitness staff of eight, coordinating, planning, and budgeting fitness activities for approximately 500 employees. When Texas-T offered him the position, both he and his wife agreed they should "jump" at the opportunity.

George was eager to impact the very first day on the job. He brought all his success stories and strategies from Honnoco and set about telling the employees that he was going to make some changes, and utilize the programs that had worked so well at Honnoco. George informed the employees of the changes in their job descriptions, hourly wages, and responsibilities. He then proceeded to change the program of fitness activities for employees. As soon as the changes were in place, George stated what his promotional and advertising strategies would entail—to assist in "getting the word out" to the corporate management and employees.

What soon followed sent George's plans into a tailspin. Employee participation in the corporate fitness program dropped from over 70 percent to a meager 22 percent. Four of the fitness staff resigned with two more additional employees threatening resignation. Employee absenteeism began to rise and productivity dropped in the manufacturing division. That's when top company management became alarmed and called in George for an explanation. He was totally confused as to what caused the turnaround of the fitness facility. Company management gave him one month to reform the programs. George resigned the next week.

DISCUSSION QUESTIONS

1. Cite some of the mistakes George made in attempting to implement Honnoco's program at Texas-T?

2. What could George have done differently in his initial assessment of the situation at Texas-T?

3. Is there only one best way to manage? George had run a successful program before. What went wrong?

■ ■ ■ ■ ■ ■ ■

There are some invaluable lessons that can be learned from the dilemma faced by George Ruggles and his management experiences of both Texas-T and Honnoco. The case in point helps to emphasize that yes, there is more than one best way to manage and there are many sport management factors that "make" or "break" a sport business.

To help assure your future success as a manager, the following chapter examines various theories of management, the levels of management, the roles managers play, skills that a manager should possess, and internal/external factors that a manager must learn to control in organizational environments. And most important of all, this chapter will show you how to avoid the management pitfalls George encountered while at Texas-T.

MANAGEMENT APPROACHES AVAILABLE TO SPORT MANAGERS

There have been, since the early 1900s, five theoretical approaches to management. Each approach builds upon the next, and will be introduced from the earliest theory or management approach to the more recent approaches to management (Schoderbek, Schoderbek, & Kefalas, 1980). The five approaches—classical, behavioral, management science, systems, and contingency—all have made unique contributions to understanding the how and why managers function as they do and collectively will help to develop your own personal sport management style.

TABLE 3.1 Sport Manager Tasks

Planning	Organizing	Controlling
Define goals and objectives Create (a "blueprint")	Design jobs for accomplishing these strategies	Assure that what was planned actually does happen
	Design organizational structure to assist in carrying out goals and objectives	Correct deviations that might have occurred as plans were implemented

The Classical Approach

Indeed, as the name indicates, this approach uses the classical management functions to explain how managers function. The basic premise of the **classical approach** is that there is a core knowledge that each manager must master. These core dimensions include mastering the functions of planning, organizing, and controlling. Table 3.1 helps to explain these three functions and how they are interrelated.

By reviewing table 3.1 and reviewing the case of George at Texas-T, George performed two of the three functions successfully. He planned out his program goals and objectives, and re-organized the fitness staff functions and hours to assist in carrying out his plans. But what ultimately happened at Texas-T *did not* match George's plan of attack. Puzzled? Read on.

The Behavioral Approach

Stimulated by findings of the Hawthorne's studies in the 1930s, this approach went beyond the original idea that all a manager did was plan, organize, and control. The classical approach ignored one important ingredient—people! Individuals respond differently according to their unique needs, wants, and desires. The Hawthorne investigation found that worker productivity improved when they were given individual attention, treated with dignity, and addressed as individuals by management. This classic experiment gave rise to the behavioral science approach. The **behavioral approach** focused on individual needs and differences. These researchers used ideas from the fields of psychology, anthropology, and sociology, which laid the foundation of the behavioral approach (Stewart, 1982).

Did George attempt to look at the fitness staff needs and Texas-T needs when redesigning programs and jobs? Did he ask for input or feedback from these people? No! Hence, the importance of understanding how to motivate, lead, and effectively communicate to people. Part III of this book examines these management skills in detail.

The Management Science Approach

The most exact and precise approach thus far, the **management science approach** set out to use the precision of statistics and mathematics to assist in managing with greater efficiency. With the advent of the computer, this approach served to impact operations management, and more specifically, manufacturing operations. This approach examines such operational problems as product or project planning and control, quality control of goods and services, employee satisfaction models, and inventory control (Gribbins & Hunt, 1988).

Again, let's refer to the example of George. If he had looked at employee satisfaction models he might have prevented the 50 percent turnover that occurred with the fitness staff at Texas-T. If George had comprehension of what typically satisfies and dissatisfies employees in the general workplace, he would have understood the importance of asking for employee's input about the programming and job design changes he implemented.

The Systems Approach

The **systems approach** built on the three previous approaches by recognizing that the more precise you can predict how the system as a whole will function, the more successful you will manage (Kast & Rosenzweig, 1972). This idea draws from the concept that to manage effectively, you must recognize that every organization is a system that is made up of integrated parts. To be successful, one must recognize that all parts must function as a whole to meet the objectives of an organization.

Getting back to George, he should have realized if the fitness staff wasn't happy, the employees participating in the corporate fitness program wouldn't be happy either. This, in turn, led to management's unhappiness with George's work performance and to the lack of subsequent support for George's ideas. Recognizing all of the needs of the various parts as they contributed to the successful operation of the organization as a whole would have made the difference at Texas-T.

The Contingency Approach

The **contingency approach** supports the notion that to manage effectively, there is no "one best" way to manage (Koontz, 1990). Managers must find different ways to manage different situations and recognize that there is no one best "prescription" for any organization, regardless of the nature, type, or kind of business situation. This approach goes even beyond the scope of our discussion here and provides the rationale for this textbook. The book will provide you with a variety of options, theories, or ideas to choose from when managing.

If George had realized that he could not simply transplant the ideas and program options he used at Honnoco to the company at Texas-T, he'd probably still be coordinating the program there. Sorry George, but there is no "one best" way to manage and this called for a situational analysis, and a different plan of attack!

You are now familiar with some popular management theories used by practicing sport managers. But what do sport managers really do? What are their jobs like? What other factors must they understand to manage effectively? There is *much* more to managing than these theories provide! The following section addresses these issues.

THE SPORT MANAGER'S WORKING ENVIRONMENT

Any sport organization, regardless of structure and size, must respond to a variety of internal and external forces to survive. Every manager must learn to control the changes in the **internal environment** (i.e., staff turnover, membership loss). According to Mintzberg (1978), managers must also deal with the **external environment** (i.e., economy, social, and cultural change). Table 3.2 helps to further explain the sport manager's working environment.

TABLE 3.2 Internal and External Sport Management Environments	
Internal Environment	**External Environment**
Manager Levels—lower, middle, and upper	High Tech Influences
Manager Roles—decisional (entrepreneur, disturbance handler, recourse allocator, negotiator)	Political Climate
Manager Roles—interpersonal (leader, figurehead, liaison)	Cultural/Social Factors
Manager Roles—informational (monitor, disseminator, spokesperson)	Clientele
	Competitors

External Factors

Externally and internally the sport manager must play host to a variety of factors. Externally, ever changing technological advances force the manager to constantly change the working environment and stay competitive with other sport businesses (Kirkland, 1988). With the advent of the computer and the FAX machine, managers are forced to stay abreast of high tech advances so their organizations can continue to run more effectively and efficiently.

Politics, politicians, and their subsequent impact on regulations and legislation force sport managers to comply with the ever changing legal and regulatory environment. For example, if property taxes increase, the sport managers must decide if they will pass this cost on to their respective sport consumers, or cut back on staff and/or services.

The economy can force a sport manager out of business or provide high profit margins to a club. In times of economic recession, prospective consumers are forced to tighten their belts and reduce spending. When the economy is prosperous and healthy, consumers are much more likely to purchase that health club membership or ticket to see the Seattle Seahawks.

Cultural and social factors also affect the manager's environment. For example, the types of activities that have greater appeal to consumers in the Northeast might be ice hockey, skiing, and squash. Whereas, in southern California with a milder climate, consumers might enjoy more jogging, surfing, and soccer. The manager must take these factors into consideration when scheduling activities.

And yes, the clientele does affect business operations performed by sport managers. Urban dweller needs and interests are different from those of the suburbanite. An individual's socioeconomic status also affects their purchase power and, hence, needs and interests. Managers dealing with an older consumer must gear their sales pitch or membership drive differently than they would when dealing with a younger consumer.

The type, nature, and location of one's competitors forces managers to develop their business strategies accordingly. If they have a product that sells itself, such as Boston Celtic tickets, they have an easy time marketing and promoting ticket sales. However, if they are one of four health spas in a five-mile radius, they must provide some type of unique appeal to consumers to sell memberships, such as a two-for-one promotion sale or provide a unique fitness class not available at the other health clubs.

Internal Environment Concerns

Internally, sport managers have much greater control over the environment because they make decisions over the people they hire and how they choose to react to different situational factors. Most internal environments require three levels of management—lower, middle, and upper—and each level calls for execution of different skills and roles (Gemmel, 1986). Table 3.3 helps distinguish between these levels, skills, and roles.

As table 3.3 illustrates, the *lower level manager* has more direct contact with employees and members of a health club, therefore, they must be well versed in "people" skills. They must be able to relate to and understand the unique needs of both of these groups. Additionally, they are responsible for the direct supervision of employee work. This calls for technical expertise or understanding of the skills that each employee must possess to effectively do the job. The skills required of first-level managers call for expertise as a job monitor, an effective leader of individuals. Because of the direct contact with employees and members, they are often the ones who first must handle conflict or disturbances. Hence they must be prepared to "put out the fires."

Middle managers must have the greatest interaction skill capabilities of the three levels of management. To please both upper and lower management needs or demands, the middle manager must act as a liaison, effectively disseminating information and also allocating resources (budgets) from upper management to lower management program directors.

TABLE 3.3 Levels, Skills, and Roles of Sport Managers at XYZ Health Club

Management Level	Skills	Roles
Lower Management:		
Racquet Sport Director	Human interaction Technical job expertise	Monitor Leader Disturbance handler
Middle Management:		
Assistant Club Manager	Greatest need for interaction Responds to both lower and upper management needs	Liaison Disseminator Resource Person Allocator
Upper Management:		
Club General Manager	Must see BIG picture	Entrepreneur Negotiator Spokesperson Figurehead

Source: First Introduced by Henry Mitzberg, "The Managers Job" in *Understanding Management,* p. 220, 1978, Harper & Row, New York, NY.

The *upper manager* is the club's spokesperson, risk taker, and liaison with the external environment. He/she must possess keen negotiation skills when hiring staff or negotiating with lenders for financing capital improvements.

Table 3.3 points out what a typical health club scenario might hold for a manager inside the organization. Levels, roles, and skills do vary somewhat organization to organization, but for the most part these general assumptions can be made of internal environments in health clubs. As a first-level manager you will probably require both interaction and a technical knowledge base because you direct the racquet sports staff. You need to positively interact with these people and effectively evaluate their performance. The roles you will likely have to perform at this level include monitoring performance, leading staff, and conflict resolution arising between staff and/or members.

As a middle manager you become the typical "go between" for top management and lower management. You must possess very effective interaction skills because you are trying to make everyone happy. Therefore, the role that is important to your success includes becoming a management liaison between upper and lower levels, disseminating important information from upper management to lower and feedback from lower managers to upper on how things at the "grass roots" are coming along. You will more than likely be responsible for budget assessment and development for the various program directors; hence, your role as a resource allocator comes into play. Finally, you negotiate for the final approval on most hiring decisions, programs, and club operating budgets. You also must negotiate these decisions with club ownership.

As the general manager, your focus is to constantly balance the external forces in the environment and the internal reactions to these factors. This is known as "seeing the BIG picture." You have to contend with club ownerships needs, wants, and demands. You must be a broad-visioned person and keep everything in perspective. What roles are necessary to do this? You must be an entrepreneur, balancing the risky external environment and your creative and innovative responses to these changes. You are also a spokesperson, representing the club in your local community events and/or speaking engagements.

SUMMARY

1. There are five major approaches to the study of management. These include the classical approach, behavioral approach, management science approach, systems approach, and contingency approach.
2. The sport manager must be aware of both the internal and external environmental factors that influence successful operations.
3. External factors include the economy, technology, politics, competition, clientele, and social and cultural factors.
4. Internal factors important to managers include job levels, skills, and roles.
5. There are three levels of management in any organization: lower, middle, and upper.
6. Each management level calls for either technical, human, or conceptual skills from a manager.
7. There are several categories of roles a sport manager must perform—interpersonal, decisional, and informational.

REVIEW QUESTIONS

1. There is no one best way to manage. What is meant by this statement?
2. Choose any approach to the study of management and defend its usefulness to the practice of modern-day sport management.
3. How do all three management levels contribute in the work environment?
4. Many people believe that being an entrepreneur is the most important role that any manager performs. Do you agree or disagree? Explain.

Louisiana Superdome
New Orleans, Louisiana

Proactive Planning Strategies That Work

■ ■ ■ ■ ■ ■ ■

CASE STUDY
Who Ever Heard of Planning Anyway?

Rita Rodinie insisted that her job was nothing but crisis management in her five years of managing the concession operations for the Extravaganza Dome in Las Vegas, Nevada. One day, five years ago, after topping all the hot dog sales at concessions booth #2 during an Ice Capades event, her boss pleaded with her to take over management of concessions so he could assume another position in the front office. He had seen her perform capably as an employee over the last year and thought she could easily manage the concessions operations. Excited, Rita agreed to give it a try. It is very interesting to learn what soon transpired.

Through Rita's efforts, concessions became a gold mine for the Extravaganza Dome Operating Company. With a relatively small staff of twenty-five, concession sales doubled during the first year and continued to escalate thereafter. At first glance, one would think that Rita was some kind of terrific sport manager. Perhaps not. Let's examine the situation.

No other concession company was allowed in the dome and spectators were not allowed to bring any food or drinks into the facility. Rita essentially had no competition. The food was better than average and not as overpriced as concession stands in other arenas tend to be. Rita's claim to fame was, "Everyone knows our reputation of quality and you just can't beat my tasty foot-long hot dogs anywhere! No one can compare! Even if we raise the price, these dogs are always going to sell!"

When asked what planning strategies made her so successful, she had some interesting comments.

"I don't ever plan. Wouldn't think of it. Just too much trouble and nothin' ever turns out the way you think it will anyway. Sales just keep going up and there are really no cycles in the concession business. These people come in here and part of their wonderful time is the opportunity to try my lip-smackin' concessions. I don't really plan the inventory; the concession salespeople just kind of know when to drop by. Our goals are to make a million by the year 2000. I really don't have to train employees. Whenever anyone quits, we just hire new ones, and they learn by watching or asking questions."

DISCUSSION QUESTIONS

1. *Does Rita plan?*
2. *With that kind of successful sales record, is Rita an effective sport manager?*
3. *Would planning help the concessions business at Extravaganza operate more effectively?*

■ ■ ■ ■ ■ ■ ■

WHY PLAN?

As ridiculous as it may seem, some managers fail to see the inherent value in planning. They consider it a waste of time, wishful thinking, or something that only works in textbooks. Then again, most of these types are not as effective as they could be. Furthermore, was Rita actually planning? Let's examine some facts about planning and, hence, the importance of being proactive as a sport manager.

Facts about Planning

Planning prepares the organization for change. If there is anything that sport managers can predict about future events it is that change is inevitable: the economy will change; the demand for fitness services will change; the type of customer they might attract could change; competing sport businesses might come and go. The prepared manager will be proactive to these changes by establishing different plans for different economical climates or various business strategies if the demand for services decreases or increases. Rita's management approaches certainly did not address the possibility of change. She would have to react to these changes after the fact and more than likely lose profits in the meantime.

Planning reduces organizational conflict. If employees and management agree on a plan of attack, they will be less confused over what their job expectations might be. Budgets will be easier to justify because workers will see the reasons for expenditures. Wouldn't Rita's employee training be more effective if, for example, they had a training manual outlining their performance objectives, as opposed to just watching other employees or interrupting their work by asking questions, causing possible conflict.

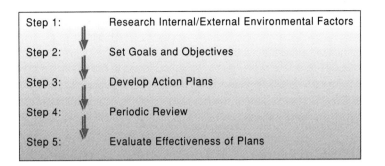

FIGURE 4.1
Essential elements of
planning.

Planning helps to increase work efficiency in organizations by reducing overlapping and wasteful activities. By establishing priorities and time frames for organizational plans, the sport manager will more likely see a happy and productive environment. Employees will know what is expected of them, especially when they become directly involved in the planning process. If Rita's employees knew what kind of sales volume they must generate in concessions and were rewarded for meeting expectations, Rita would likely see improvements in employee performance *and* profits.

WHAT IS PLANNING?

The planning concept should not be new to you. If you recall in chapter 3, original studies of management elaborated on the three basic tasks that managers perform: planning, organizing, and controlling. Planning can be defined as a management function which establishes goals and objectives and the means by which they can be achieved (Harris, 1983). Planning should spell out what you want to accomplish in an organization, how you will accomplish the task, and an appropriate means of measuring whether the objectives have been met. All sport managers are directly responsible for developing plans for their organization. They may be short range (less than one year) or long range (one to five years) (Roman, 1987). What does it take to develop a sport business plan? Figure 4.1 gives you the essential elements in the planning process: research internal and external environments, establish objectives, develop strategic planning, periodic review, and evaluation.

ESSENTIAL ELEMENTS OF PLANNING

Research Environments

As you may recall in chapter 3, you were given internal and external factors that affect a manager's job. Now you are ready to see some specific reasons why. You must ask a variety of research questions about your environment to develop achievable objectives. For example, is the economy healthy so that your business will thrive? Will people have the money to purchase your particular service or product? Who are your competitors and do you have the capability to "outgun" them? Are the social and cultural needs and expectations such that people will buy your product (i.e., opening a surf shop in Dallas, Texas might be a poor business decision, but perfectly reasonable in Malibu, California)? Politically and legally speaking, are there government regulations or legal issues that force you to design your business in a certain fashion? And finally, do you have the financial and physical resources to establish and/or continue the operation of your business (i.e., do you have the money and the person-power to make your plan achievable?).

Establish Objectives

This is one of the most critical steps in the planning process. **Objectives** must be achievable, measurable, realistic, and motivating. Most of all, the people who are responsible for achieving them must align their work behavior with the accomplishment of the objectives.

How does the effective manager assure that all these objective criterion are met? Peter Drucker, in 1954, introduced a wonderful way to establish objectives in his *management-by-objectives* (MBO) theory. Peter believed that objectives will be achievable, realistic, and motivating if established concurrently by management and employees. If all parties agree on objectives they must strive for, the likelihood of the objective actually being carried out is greater. Through mutual discussions, management and employees establish individual and unit goals, which are directly aligned with what the organization wants to accomplish. For example, rather than management demand that a racket sports instructor teach 20 beginning tennis classes per week, both management and the instructor agree on what the demand for instruction is and how many classes the instructor can effectively and efficiently teach per week.

TABLE 4.1 Effective Decision Making: Selecting the Right Job for You!

A's Weights		B's Weights	
Advancement	= 10	Salary	= 10
Opportunities for spouse	= 7	Firm's reputation	= 7
Salary	= 5	Security	= 5
Firm's reputation	= 4	Advancement	= 4
Cost of living	= 3	Cost of living	= 3
Climate	= 2	Opportunities for spouse	= 2
Security	= 1	Climate	= 1

Equally important to the objective setting stage is effective **decision making.** Prioritizing objectives is a difficult task and making a decision always involves a certain amount of uncertainty (Simon, 1960). To help you effectively make decisions you must:

- Ascertain the need to make a decision (e.g., choosing between accepting a job with one health club or the other).
- Establish decision criteria. (Using the job choice decision, your criteria might be: opportunities for advancement; opportunities for spouse, if married; salary; firm's reputation; cost of living; climate; and job security.)
- Allocate weights to criterion. (Depending on personal priorities, person "A" may weigh criteria differently than person "B". In table 4.1, person "A" is more concerned about advancement and a spouse's happiness. Whereas, person "B" is more concerned with money, the firm's reputation, and security issues.)
- Compare your alternatives. (Which job is better?)
- Evaluate your alternatives. (Why is that job better?)
- Select the best alternative. (Based on your weights and deductive reasoning capabilities, which decision makes the most sense?)

These suggested decision-making tools help to guide your effectiveness as a manager and make prioritizing objectives easier.

Strategic Planning

Objectives are meaningless unless they are incorporated into an "action plan" which provides direction for the operation of your business. **Strategic planning** allows for your objectives to be converted into direct action and implemented at operational levels. This is a relatively easy process and regardless of the nature of your business, it typically consists of: a mission statement, organizational objectives, organizational strategies, and a business portfolio plan (Koontz, 1976).

The Mission Statement

The **mission statement** is your broad, visionary business focus which explains what you want to accomplish with your business and what distinguishes your business from others. It should be revised AT LEAST every five years to keep pace with changes that might occur in your internal environment or external environment (Raia, 1974). It should focus on target markets, be achievable, and be realistic. Three sample mission statements for the different sport segments are given below:

> *Consumer Segment*: To develop and market mutually beneficial concession food products for the consumer and concession operator.
>
> *Spectator Segment*: To provide a selected range of quality events to fulfill spectator's entertainment needs and interests.
>
> *Participant Segment*: To provide healthy, well-organized sporting events that allow for fulfilling sporting experiences to the participant.

Organizational Objectives

Organizational objectives are more detailed statements derived from your business's mission statement (Lawrence & Osborn, 1981). They should be able to be converted into specific plans and provide details for department operational plans. Using the above mission statements, let's tack on some organizational objectives so you can see the connection in the strategic planning process, as seen in table 4.2.

TABLE 4.2 Sample Objectives in the Consumer, Spectator, and Participant Industry Segments

	Consumer	Spectator	Participant
Profit	Increase market share by 20%	Have 4 sell-out events per season	Have over 50% of corporate employees participate
Growth	Add another racquet production plant	Develop arena for corporate sponsors	Add a free weight room for member use
Market Penetration	Market a racquet to appeal to both the beginner and advanced tennis player, rather than only advanced	Market event so it appeals to all ages, not just college-age spectators	Demonstrate that both males and females benefit from weight training, not just males
Leadership	We want our golf ball to be the #1 played ball among tour pros	They want our pro tennis tour to attract record attendance	We want our marathon to attract more participants than any other road race
Client Satisfaction	To assure that our customers are satisfied with each jogging shoe they purchase	To provide our members with satisfying event experiences	To make our members feel important every time they visit our club
Productivity	To increase the number of shoe contracts with retail outlets by 10%	Reduce overhead in our sport facility by 10%	Improve the quality of teaching by the racquet sports instructor
Social	To reduce pollution controls in the ball manufacturing plant by 25%	Make building modifications to assure accessibility for the handicapped	To provide free cholesterol testing for members in the community and in the club

TABLE 4.3 Organizational Strategy Options		
	Present Services/ Products	**New Services/Products**
Present Clients	Market Penetration	Product/Service Development
New Clients	Market Development	Diversification

Organizational Strategies

Organizational strategies are your grand design for achieving your organizational objectives. They tend to either concentrate on present customers or find new customers, or present products/services or introduce new products/services. The four possibilities, of which you may choose to adopt one or all four, include market penetration, market development, product/service development, or diversification (Schendel, Patton, & Riggs, 1976). Table 4.3 elaborates on these strategies and how they change as a business matures.

As denoted in table 4.3, a sport business will target a particular group of individuals or a "market" to whom they wish to sell their product or service. This is called *market penetration*; for example, targeting all college-age students with your membership drive at a health club through your sales and promotions campaigns.

Market development is another business strategy directed at attracting new clientele. By attracting new customers you can increase profits or replace exhausted markets. Using the health club example, this strategy not only targets college-age students but allows you to target middle-aged adults, as well as individuals ages 25–40.

A product or service development strategy takes existing target markets and introduces new services or products to them. Again, returning to the health club scenario, use your original customers, and introduce new weight training equipment or a new fitness class to help existing members or attract new college-age students.

Diversification is the most financially risky of the business strategies. With diversification, you are marketing a new service or product to new customers. It requires additional monies to purchase new products and new advertising strategies aimed at new clientele. Anytime you attempt to take

TABLE 4.4 Corporate Fitness Business Portfolio Matrix

Market Share

		High	Low
Market Growth	**High**	Star (Low-Impact Aerobics)	Question Mark (Jogging Track)
	Low	Cash Cow (Weight Room)	Cash Trap (Racquetball Courts)

on new clientele by introducing new products or services, there is no guarantee you will succeed in winning them over! Hence, diversification is by far the most complicated planning strategy a sport manager could choose.

Most businesses begin their organizational strategy by targeting a small number of markets with a few products or services they feel will be successful. As the business grows and profits increase, they can afford to advertise to other target markets or offer new products or services. When a business becomes comfortable with existing clientele and business offerings, they then might attempt to diversify. Much of the rationale for choosing one strategy over the other is rooted in the mission and objectives of a business.

Business Portfolios

Finally, an organization's strategic planning process culminates with the designation of a business portfolio. A portfolio attempts to specifically designate programs or "standard business units" (SBUs) according to their market share and market growth potential. Each program of SBU falls into one of four categories, based on their market share and growth potential. This kind of portfolio matrix helps you to decide which programs you might want to build or invest in. The portfolio may suggest a delay in decision making until the coming quarter in terms of market share and growth. Finally, it might suggest elimination of a program that is not carrying an adequate share of the market and has no potential to do so (MacMillan, Hambrick, & Day, 1982). Table 4.4 outlines these four categories—*Star, Question Mark, Cash Cow, Cash Trap*—in a business portfolio matrix and provides sample programs found in the corporate fitness industry.

As you can observe from our example of a corporate fitness club, specific programs or SBUs are categorized according to market share and growth potential. Low-impact aerobics is the most popular program, attracting the greatest number of participants and these numbers continue to increase on a weekly basis. For these reasons, low-impact aerobics is labeled a "star." Next, the weight room facility is classified as a "cash cow" because the high number of participants consistently using this program. The "question mark," the jogging track, has seen a steady rise in number of participants; however, it is not near the consistency or growth that the low-impact aerobics and weight room programs have shown, hence, a question mark. Finally, numbers have continued to drop in participant use of the racquetball courts, therefore this program is labeled a "cash trap."

This particular business portfolio tells the sport manager to increase funding and/or staff in the low-impact aerobic program because of its obvious popularity. The cash cow weight room should continue on its present course; funding should be steady because of the consistent popularity of this program. The fitness track should be watched closely. Most managers would only commit to short-term funding until the growth share can be determined. Finally, the astute manager would eliminate the racquetball program. The racquetball courts could be renovated into low-impact aerobic studios. The participation numbers do not justify expenditures on this program.

By using the strategic planning process, managers can put plans into action. They can implement their mission statements and organizational objectives into specific marketing strategies. The effectiveness of your strategy selection can be tested in examining a program's relative position on the portfolio matrix. You also can gain valuable feedback as to whether mission statements and objectives are realistic and achievable.

Periodic Review and Evaluation

The final steps in any plan are to periodically review and evaluate progress made toward completing established objectives. It assures that objectives are realistic and achievable by a sport business. How does one evaluate a plan's effectiveness? An organization should assess progress made to objective achievement on a weekly, monthly, quarterly, semi-annually, and yearly basis. This type of periodic review helps to assure that stated objectives do, indeed, become realistic. (Rita, I hope you're listening.)

SUMMARY

1. Planning helps the sport manager offset change, increase efficiency, and provide direction for employees.
2. The planning process consists of five basic steps: research the internal and external environments, establish objectives, strategic planning, periodic review, and evaluation.
3. Objectives should be realistic, achievable, and measurable.
4. An organization's objectives are set into motion with the assistance of a strategic plan. This plan should consist of a mission statement, organizational objectives, organizational strategies, and a business portfolio plan.
5. Periodic review and evaluation of plans are critical to successful planning efforts. This should take place on a weekly, monthly, quarterly, semi-annual, and annual basis.

REVIEW QUESTIONS

1. Why plan? Explain.
2. There are objectives common to all organizations. Is this statement true or false? Why?
3. Organizational objectives are the end points of the mission statement. Explain.
4. Decision making is critical to objective setting. Why?
5. How can you relate MBO (management-by-objectives) to the total planning process?
6. What role does the strategic planning process play in the planning process?
7. How might Rita Rodinie benefit from the planning process? Give a detailed response.

How to Get Organized

■ ■ ■ ■ ■ ■ ■

CASE STUDY
Is This Any Way to Run a Company?

Doug Blocker had been the communication coordinator for Top Flyer Golf Division for two years. His job responsibilities included sending out news releases to the media, compiling and developing company newsletters, keeping track of media coverage, and developing golf ball advertising campaigns. During his two years with the company, Doug had seen the organization of the company slowly erode away. Top Flyer had merged with Foot Comfort Golf Shoes and entire divisions were combined or deleted at the CEO's whim. For example, corporate communications of Top Flyer Marketing Division and Foot Comfort Marketing Division were combined into one division, to serve both companies' communication needs. There was total confusion over who was heading what division. To top it all, the CEO of Top Flyer/Foot Comfort refused to release any of the merger information to the press, so Doug was forced to handle each company as separate communication accounts, as if the merger had never occurred.

One morning at 8 A.M. Doug had finally had enough. He had just received a communiqué from Mary Sue Buffet, Vice President of Corporate Communications, requesting he send out separate newsletters, as planned, to the employees of both Foot Comfort and Top Flyer. Doug then proceeded to call the printer requesting both print jobs. Dedra, the printer, informed him there was only enough money budgeted for one newsletter. The head of marketing for Foot Comfort then called to say they had just mailed the newly printed company newsletter out to their employees and would he like a copy for his files. Irate, Doug stormed into Mary Sue's office and demanded to know what was happening. Why had he spent countless hours developing and proofing two newsletters when Foot Comfort had duplicated his efforts by developing and mailing their own newsletter? Emphatically Doug screamed, "Mary Sue, is this any way to run a company?" Doug left the company one week later and now sells insurance.

DISCUSSION QUESTIONS

 1. *Is there a formal chain of command at Top Flyer/Foot Comfort?*
 2. *What could Mary Sue have done to improve conditions?*
 3. *Did Doug have other options than quitting his job?*

■ ■ ■ ■ ■ ■ ■

GETTING IN THE FLOW—CHARTING AND ORGANIZING FOR SUCCESS

How does one avoid Doug's dilemma? Doug, believe it or not, is not unlike many employees in disorganized or poorly managed companies that have unsuccessfully structured their business. So why is effective organization of department and jobs critical to efficient operations in sport management? The following section should help you to learn how to organize for success.

ORGANIZING DEFINED

Organizing maximizes performance levels of your employees by defining their functional jobs or tasks, allocating these jobs to appropriately sized department units, and defining the authority and power relationships of these units. If done properly, the organizing function helps to assure clear-cut lines of responsibility and provides smooth and uninterrupted communication flow.

As you can see, Top Flyer Golf Division accomplished none of the above. Work and responsibilities were duplicated and not adequately defined. Communication was poor between the marketing division of Foot Comfort and the corporate communication division. The CEO (chief executive officer) of the company did not share his reasons for restructuring both companies. Obviously, organizing for efficient flow of operations requires top to bottom commitment in any organization. To understand the organizing function to its fullest starts with the smallest but most important unit in any organization, defining jobs of your employees. The following section will help you design motivational jobs for your employees.

CREATING EFFECTIVE JOBS

The key to designing jobs effectively lies in balancing work responsibilities and productivity. Top Flyer Golf Division, for example, failed to restructure job definitions at both Top Flyer and Foot Comfort. The end result was loss of productivity, duplication of responsibilities, and job turnover, resulting in loss of a valued employee. How does one balance the job design for employees? Let's examine several suggestions by tracing the historical development of job design in the United States.

Initially, jobs were classified by two simple divisions of labor, white collar and blue collar workers. This assessment of job design was very appropriate for job design during the industrial era around the turn of the twentieth century. White collar was designated as management who supervised blue collar workers who worked primarily on the assembly line (Carlyle, 1988).

As jobs, manufacturing, and corporations became more sophisticated, there was greater need for defining job tasks and responsibilities. Jobs were defined during the 1930s and 1940s into further categories of depth and scope. Job depth was the variety of job responsibilities assigned to a worker and the scope referred to the time frame a worker was expected to complete a task. Typically, the lower in the organization workers were, the less freedom of duties they had or less responsibility they possessed. The lower structured worker also had less job depth.

Revolutionary new strategies for job design were then introduced in the 1960s and 1970s. Hackman, Oldham, Janson, and Purdy introduced the "five core dimensions" for job design. These dimensions included task variety, identity, significance, autonomy, and feedback (1975).

Task variety addressed job fulfillment. Workers want and expect a variety of tasks during their daily job routine. Hackman, Oldham, Janson, and Purdy found workers to be less motivated when they placed the same part in the same piece of machinery hour after hour, day after day.

Also important is *task identity*. This job dimension allows a worker to identify with a complete piece of work, for example, identifying with a finished racquet or golf ball, or developing a new aerobics program from start to finish and seeing it positively impact members at a health club.

Task significance is equally important as a core dimension. Workers should feel they are significantly impacting, through individual job contributions, to the successful operation of a sport organization. Successful food sales at a concession booth greatly contribute to the financial prosperity of an arena-operating company. The employees involved with the concessions feel that they are significantly contributing to the overall successful operation of the facility.

Autonomy is considered by many managers to be the most important core dimension. It encourages entrepreneurship in each worker, allowing workers to be creative or to be able to take risks by introducing new ideas or projects.

Finally, *task feedback* is the final dimension of job design. Every worker should receive feedback about job performance. Task feedback helps to assure motivated and productive employees. Feedback also keeps employees on line with the management-by-objectives (MBO) planning process by aligning employees with organizational and individual objectives.

It is evident that jobs differ from organization to organization. Determining why they differ, how they differ, and how individual jobs are assigned to specific departments is the next step of the organizing function performed by managers. The following section will provide you with answers to these questions.

WHAT DEPARTMENT?

How does one respond to this question? Could Doug, Mary Sue, and Top Flyer's CEO have benefitted from some prior knowledge on how to structure departments and jobs within departments?

There are several options available for managers who are implementing new programs or simply restructuring existing departments. The options can be categorized into *external focused departments* or *internal focused* (McClenahan, 1988). Let's begin with the external focused.

External Focused Departments

Sport organizations with **external focused departments** fall into three broad categories: product, customer, or geographic. Let's begin with a product-based department structure, for example, Reebok International. Their departments are product based. This structure was chosen for Reebok because of the unique product diversification or variety of their sporting goods manufacturing (see figure 5.1). The departments of Reebok are structured according to products produced because of the specialized skills required of employees to effectively assure the successful manufacturing of products or product lines.

A sport business might choose to organize departments according to the particular customer served. Figure 5.2 is an example of a customer-based external focused organization.

The last of the external focused departments is geographic. This type of department is seen most frequently with large national or international sport organizations that cover a broad geographic area. An example of this organizational structure is shown in figure 5.3.

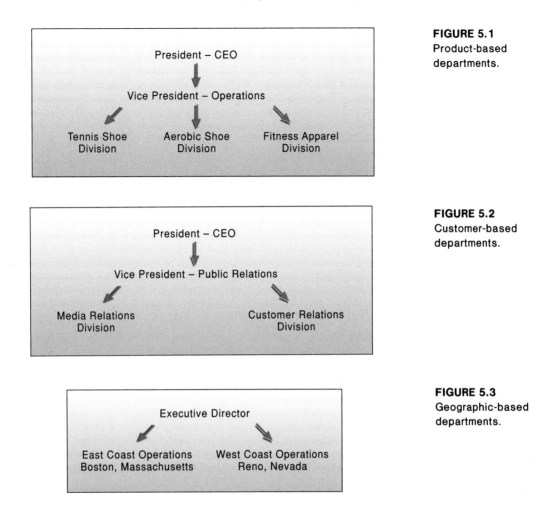

FIGURE 5.1
Product-based departments.

FIGURE 5.2
Customer-based departments.

FIGURE 5.3
Geographic-based departments.

There are advantages and disadvantages with external focused departments. Frequently, organizational strategies and objectives are easier to define because they are aligned with the mission of the company, i.e., to sell more shoes or service more customers. However, external focused departments are not always in the best interest of the internal operating environment. For example, a tennis shoe production department may lose sight of the importance of being a "team player" and not take into account the needs and interests of other departments.

Internal Focused Departments

As the name implies, **internal focused departments** target internal organization operations. There are two general classifications of internal focused departments, *process* or *functional,* that managers typically utilize. Managers must ask, "Which is most appropriate for my business and why choose these organizational structures rather than external focused options?" The following section addresses these issues.

Process and Functional Departments

Process departments are organized in accordance with the specialized job activities required to complete a given task. Sporting goods equipment manufacturers most frequently divide labor along these lines. Figure 5.4 provides you with an example of a racquet manufacturing company.

In contrast, *functional departments* are organized by specific functions. This is the most frequently used method of departmentalizing jobs in the sport industry. An example of this type of structure can be seen in figure 5.5.

Both functional and process departments focus on employee skills. This focus makes worker job descriptions easier to develop. However, sometimes these structures tend to ignore the forces in the external environment because of the internal focus. Managers have a more difficult time of coordinating all the specialized work units in an internal focused organizational structure.

What criteria should you use in deciding which department best fits your sport business? There are some guidelines for department selection, first introduced by Kalzn in 1982.

- Which selection best uses the technical expertise of employees?
- Which selection allows for the most efficient and effective use of office equipment or machinery?
- Which allows the manager to best coordinate and control operations of employees?

Sizing Up Departments

Now that you have defined departments and specific jobs, how do you determine department size? From the perspective of a manager, do you require a wide or narrow span of control over the employees you are

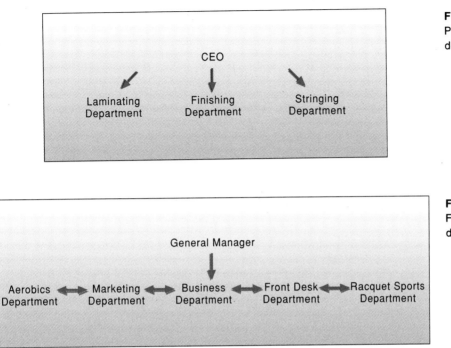

FIGURE 5.4
Process
departmentalization.

FIGURE 5.5
Function
departmentalization.

supervising? (Hall, 1986). A wide span of control places more jobs under one manager, and conversely, a narrow span specifies fewer jobs under one manager. A wider span of control allows for less individual employee contact by the supervisor, however, communication is usually more effective because more individuals report to one manager. To assist you in determining how large or small your span of control should be, use the following suggestions:

- If your employees are very specialized in their job function, use a narrow span of control.
- If you have a lot of experience as a manager, usually you can choose a wide span of control.
- If your employees are seasoned veterans, use a wider span of control.
- The physical proximity of your employees will also assist you in size, selection, and natural groupings of departments.

TABLE 5.1 Flowchart Design: XYZ Sport Franchise

	Team Owner	
Personnel Office	General Manager	Administrative Assistant
Head Coach	Marketing/Public Relations Director	Business Office Manager
5 Assistant Coaches		
Head Athletic Trainer	Assistant Marketing/PR Director	Accountant
		Ticket Manager, Payroll
Players/2 Asst. Trainers	Marketing/PR Interns	Business Interns

CHAIN OF COMMAND: DEFINING POWER AND AUTHORITY RELATIONSHIPS WITHIN YOUR ORGANIZATION

Your next major hurdle in organizing your sport business is delineating power and authority relationships. Chain of command refers to the top-to-bottom hierarchy in any organization. By defining the chain of command, all employees and managers are aware of who they report to or are responsible for supervising.

There are several rules of thumb when organizing the chain of command, frequently referred to as a "flowchart." Never have a person report to more than one manager or supervisor. This leads to problems in communication and defining job responsibilities. Typically, individuals at the top of the flowchart carry the most power and authority, which decreases as one goes down the flowchart. Individuals on the same horizontal line carry the same amount of power and responsibility in their job and should never report to each other, but instead to those above them on the chart. Vertical lines proceeding from a department or individual usually indicate a staff position that serves to support the line department or individual—secretaries and adminstrative positions usually serve in staff capacities. Finally, certain departments, such as payroll or the personnel office, carry responsibilities to all employees. A more detailed picture of flowchart structure and requirements is provided for you in the hypothetical sport franchise in table 5.1.

Power and Authority: When to Delegate It and When Not to!

Max Weber, first to examine authority relationships in organizations proposed that authority is vested in the position one holds. Therefore, the job description outlining job responsibilities insinuates that the employee also has the authority to carry out those responsibilities. Why do some employees then have trouble defining or using the authority vested in their position? Or better yet, why do many secretaries possess more authority than they should? Both provide examples of misused authority. To prevent these situations, remember the following key points when defining authority relations in any sport business:

- Employees must be willing to accept their superiors' authority. If they don't respect the superior or doubt their authority, they might choose to reject requests from that superior.
- Employees must be able to understand what is expected of them. If expectations are unclear, they might ignore the request or respond incorrectly to management demand.
- What a superior asks employees to perform must be consistent with the goals of the organization.
- Employees must be physically and mentally capable of carrying out the request.
- Outline clear and concise flowcharts to prevent employees from overstepping authority boundaries.

Power versus Authority

These two terms are frequently confused. **Authority,** already discussed, is defined in an employee's position. For example, an employee might possess the authority to evaluate any staff that might assist them with their work, as defined in their job description. **Power,** on the other hand, is the ability of people to influence others. When balanced properly, power and authority are equal job components and give superiors the right to make requests of subordinates. This type of job position power is legitimate. However, there are other types of power, both good and bad, that cause individuals to abuse their power in organizations. These types include coercive, reward, expert, and referent power (Keichell, 1988).

Coercive power refers to the power to cause fear or panic in others. For example, police cars equipped with radar when present cause fear in motor vehicle operators. You tend to respect their presence by slowing down. Thus they exert coercive power over you by causing you to change your driving behavior.

Reward power is the compatibility individuals reward others for behaving or acting a certain way. Let's look at the patrol car example again. If you slow down and obey the speed limit, you are rewarded not by receiving tickets, but by reducing your risk of accidents and keeping your insurance premiums at a minimum. Teachers are another example of individuals who possess reward power by awarding good grades to students who excel on an assignment or in a course.

With *expert power,* you give power to individuals you feel are "experts" in their fields. Ken Cooper for example, is highly respected in the fitness field for his contribution to the exercise and fitness theories, reducing heart attack, stress levels, etc. Therefore, many people place considerable power and respect in what he has to say about trends in the fitness industry.

The final type of power is *referent power.* We all have heroes or mentors in our lives that we respect for their accomplishments and contributions to society. We are influenced by their actions and place a certain amount of power in these actions. That explains why companies like Reebok and Nike pay professional athletes to endorse their products. Many young people today consider these athletes to be their role models and heroes and, hence, are influenced by them when it comes to buying tennis or basketball shoes.

Delegating Responsibilities

Many sport managers find themselves asking, "Do I delegate a job responsibility or do I do the job myself?" The answer depends on many factors: the capabilities of the person you are delegating work to; the appropriateness of the situation; and/or the type of request—certain management situations call for variations in delegation.

What are the advantages and disadvantages of delegating? The following section will provide some answers.

Advantages of Delegating

Delegating encourages decision making in employees and allows them to impact the operation of the business environment. This increases job satisfaction and job fulfillment.

Delegating helps to create a productive work environment. If employees feel they have more control over their job environment, they might exert greater job effort.

Delegating allows managers to devote their own work time to more essential work responsibilities. This results in a more focused job effort, eliminating the feeling that they "have to do everything or it simply won't get done."

Disadvantages of Delegating

Typically, delegating responsibilities requires further job training of those who are given these new responsibilities. This creates more work for the manager.

Delegating requires additional planning by managers to assure that certain steps are carried out and that employees who have been delegated these new responsibilities report back. Once again, it requires additional time from the manager's work day.

Managers hate to delegate because they fear a loss of authority and power. This fear often stems from lack of confidence in either oneself as a manager or from lack of trust in employees. In either case, investigating the causes of why one might fear a loss of power or authority will ultimately make a working environment for all parties.

When deciding when to delegate responsibilities, if the job environment permits, the advantages typically outweigh the disadvantages. It promotes job autonomy in employees and allows them to feel more like a team player, which, more than likely, will enhance their job satisfaction.

ORGANIZATIONAL DESIGN

So far we've discussed job design, department structuring, spans of control, authority versus power, and decisions regarding delegating responsibility. What's missing? How does it all fit together? The answer lies in your understanding important criterion used when designing your successful sport organization. The following discussion addresses essential ingredients of division of labor, centralized authority, and structure complexity used in organizational design.

DESIGN THEORIES

There are two schools of thought when it comes to selecting the best design fit for your club or sport organization, the *universalistic approach* and *contingency approach* (Mintzberg, 1979).

Universalistic Approach

The universalistic approach outlines two ways to design organizations, *classical* and *neoclassical*. The **classical design theory** is sometimes referred to as the *mechanistic approach* because its derivations came from the industrial era of assembly line and machine manufacturing of the early 1900s. The mechanistic view believes that all organizations should be designed with a well-defined division of labor, very centralized authority (delegating was taboo), and unity of command (workers report to only one supervisor).

Neoclassical design theory basically takes the opposite stand, claiming the best way to design organizations is to create internal environments with low centralization, complexity, and low formalization. Many refer to this approach as the *organic approach,* because much of the success of this type of design rests on individual workers and departments and their ability to individually respond to the changes and unique challenges of the work environment; hence, a more organic or human base.

Contingency Approach

The contingency approach claims that two factors, technology and the environment, impact how you develop organization design. If environments are stable and the technology used in those environments is also stable, then you should choose the classical design approach. If the technology is rapidly changing and the environment turbulent, one should select a neoclassical design. For example, an established sporting goods manufacturing company would choose the classical approach because of the mechanical, predictable nature of their business. Whereas, health clubs tend to select more of a neoclassical approach because they are constantly dealing with change in technology (better exercise equipment) and change in the environment (economic recession, new competition). Technology is critical to their business survival.

A final word to the wise. As sport manager you have ultimate authority and are ultimately responsible for the actions of your employees. Therefore, designing effective jobs, departments, flowcharts, and delineating and delegating power and authority relationships skillfully all help to create the "key" to your success as a manager.

SUMMARY

1. Organizing is the second work function (planning is the first) that sport managers perform. It involves coordination of jobs, departments, chain of command, delegating power and authority relationships, and defining organizational structure.
2. Jobs can be defined in terms of scope and depth. More recent ideas on job design include five core dimensions: task variety, identity, significance, autonomy, and feedback.
3. There are two classifications of department types: external focused and internal focused. External focused departments can be structured geographically, by the customer served or by the product manufactured. Internal focused departments include functional and process departments.
4. The chain of command defines power and authority relationships in organizations, with individuals on top established in the most powerful position down to the lowest level in the chain retaining the least amount of power in the organization.
5. Authority is a right and lies in the job position. Power is the ability to influence others.
6. Delegating has advantages and disadvantages. If performed correctly, delegating responsibilities to others can greatly enhance the effective operation of organizations.
7. There are two schools of thought when it comes to organizational design: universalistic and contingency approaches.

REVIEW QUESTIONS

1. The organizing function directly relates to the planning function. How?
2. Blue collar and white collar job definitions no longer have a place in modern organizational makeup. Explain this statement.
3. Internal focused departments are more efficient than external focused departments. Do you agree or disagree with this statement?
4. Successful managers should establish a balance between power and authority relationships in departments. Why?
5. Many managers hate to delegate responsibility. Why?
6. The contingency design theory has been popularized by modern-day managers. Compare the advantages and disadvantages of the contingency design approach to the universalistic design approach.

Another Control Issue

■ ■ ■ ■ ■ ■ ■

CASE STUDY
"Out-of-Control" Is "In Control"!

Holly Beth Rothchild certainly knew what having control over your employees means—or at least she thought she knew. She had been managing a small club consulting business for three years and felt she had mastered the art of monitoring employees' performance. She approached this job in a variety of ways. She frequently listened in on employee phone calls to assure that all calls were work related. She would often re-do their assignments to make sure that everything had her "personal touch." To also maintain office control, she had one or two "spies" to monitor employee performance when she was away from the office or on the phone. She made sure that everyone in the office put in a long work day (at least twelve hours)—in other words *lunch* and *breaks* were meaningless in her workplace!

One day she noticed several of the employees gathered in the coffee room and decided it was her job to "listen in" on the conversation to assure their "hearts and minds" were into their jobs! John, one of her valued spies, was complaining to Carey, coordinator of corporate accounts. John was telling Carey that everyone was tired of how the "wicked witch" Rothchild constantly told everyone what to do. Everyone was in constant fear of being chastised or corrected by Holly Beth. John had no idea how he could explain this to Holly Beth. He feared losing his job if he corrected the boss. He ended their conversation with, "She treats us like little kids—I don't know how much more we can take! I don't know why she has such a *control* issue about her job! She needs to know how to loosen the reins!" At that point, both John and Carey rounded the corner of the coffee room to find Holly Beth glaring at the two of them in disbelief!

DISCUSSION QUESTIONS

1. *If you were Holly Beth, how would you have handled the situation with John and Carey?*

2. *What is meant by the case study title: "Out-of-Control" Is "In Control"? How should Holly Beth apply this idea when monitoring the day-to-day operations of her employees?*

3. *Do you have some better ideas on how to effectively control employees in this type of situation?*

■ ■ ■ ■ ■ ■ ■

The Holly Beth scenario points out some interesting control issues. For example, how much is too much interference from sport managers who coordinate employee performance? Should employees be given a chance to provide feedback about their direct manager? Are there more subtle forms of control techniques available to you to avoid the "wicked witch" syndrome? Let's dive into these and other interesting control issues that will be discussed in detail in this chapter.

HOW TO CONTROL TO YOUR ADVANTAGE

To put it simply, controlling as a sport manager is assuring that actual results conform to the planning and organizing ideas discussed in chapters 4 and 5. Controlling as a manager allows you to determine if you hired the right person for the job, budgeted correctly for that new tennis program at the club, structured departments correctly, or if you actually met your organization's goals and objectives. It provides you with a wonderful system of "checks and balances" which helps you to be more accountable as a sport manager. In short, it helps to assure your success!

There are three phases to the control function: preliminary, concurrent, and feedback (Ouchi, 1977). **Preliminary control** involves effective staff selection and budgeting financial resources. **Concurrent control** is performed on a day-to-day basis by monitoring daily operations. **Feedback control** is accomplished by evaluating employee performance, measuring profit levels on your financial statement, and by performing routine management audits. The following sections elaborate further on the importance of these phases.

Preliminary Control Techniques

Preliminary control is typically initiated at the beginning of a sport organization's business cycle (Beach, 1980). When practicing preliminary control measures, you attempt to establish standards which are later reinforced by concurrent and feedback control measures. One can preliminarily control human, materials, capital, and financial resources. The following sections further explain these preliminary control techniques.

Preliminary Control of Human Resources

It is always important to remember that your *most valued* resource is your employees. Your success as a manager is a direct reflection of the people you hire. Therefore, developing effective job descriptions, thoroughly searching the marketplace, and finding the right person for the job are critical preliminary control issues.

Job descriptions require careful scrutiny on the manager's part. The jobs must be thoroughly researched to ensure the inclusion of key job components as well as specific job expectations and responsibilities, to allow prospective employees the ability to successfully match their job expectations with yours.

Researching job description components can be carried out through several means—all of which should be tapped. Managers can interview employees presently in the position to discover key job components. You may also want to interview other members of the department for their input about what that employee should be responsible for. You can also contact outside firms for their input about how they have designed similar jobs. The main objective in researching a job description is to send out questionnaires to a large sample of similar sport businesses to obtain job information. Additionally, many sport business publications annually release a state of the industry report which may detail job descriptions performed by industry personnel (i.e., Club Business International or the Managed Recreation Research Report).

Once you have obtained a comprehensive overview of what the job entails, you must construct the job announcement which typically consists of the following key components:

- Job Title   (Specific title with firm)
- Job Responsibilities   (Specific job duties, performance
                                           expectations)
- Job Requirements   (Educational preparation, work
                                           experience)
- Additional Job   (Letters of recommendation, salary range,
  Information   starting date, who and where to send job
                                           application materials, Equal Opportunity
                                           Employer statement)

Table 6.1 Job Selection Choices

		Decision Choices	
		Hire	Reject
Later Job Performance	**Successful**	Correct	Type I Error
	Unsuccessful	Type II Error	Correct

The final step is then hiring the right person for the job. Advertise with appropriate sources, both internally and externally. Depending on the nature of the job and business you're advertising, you may want to send out job announcements locally, statewide, or nationally. Some common advertising avenues include: newspapers, magazines, employee referral agencies, college placement offices, job directories, or networking with other professional colleagues who might recommend solid candidates.

Searching inside your organization for candidates helps to promote job motivation and competitiveness among employees. Hiring internally gives you an employee who already possesses knowledge and experience about your business. Searching outside helps to bring in "new blood," hence, new ideas, energy, and leadership possibilities. It is recommended that a job search incorporate both types of search strategies. This approach provides you with a greater opportunity of finding the right person for that job. Once you've selected the top candidates, the interview is critical. Whoever is the lucky choice for the job must understand the goals and expectations for the job to assure a perfect match in the hire. Your job selection decision carries with it two correct job choices and two errors to watch out for. Table 6.1 explores these decision options (Erickson, 1984).

Your choices are correct if you hire someone who, indeed, performs well on the job or if you reject someone who performs poorly with another firm. You commit a Type I error if you reject someone who performs well at another firm, Type II error if you hire someone who performs poorly with your firm. The results of a poor hire can mean wasted time, money, and internal organizational conflict. A successful hire will help to meet profit margins and contribute to a positive work environment for all employees. Performing this management function effectively is CRITICAL to your success as a manager!

WARNING: Don't just hire *any* warm body looking for employment—you may get burned!

Preliminary Control of Materials

This form of precontrol opportunity for managers is most typically found in the consumer or manufacturing sector of sport management. Most manufacturers will attempt to control manufacturing defects in balls, shoes, etc. by statistically sampling manufactured goods. An acceptable level for defects in materials is 3 percent of total manufactured materials. Anything above the 3 percent level indicates errors in labor or parts. This indicates too much waste is occurring in the manufacturing process. Naturally, anything under 3 percent indicates greater efficiency and profit levels in the manufacturing process. Japanese manufacturers rank high in this control area with reject levels averaging .005 percent. Many American companies have carefully examined Japanese manufacturing techniques to help remain competitive in the sporting goods manufacturing industry (Bringham, 1986).

Preliminary Control of Capital

Capital purchases are typically purchases greater than $1,000. Because these purchases are sizeable, the money-conscious sport manager must be careful of large financial commitments. Two precontrol techniques used by managers to assist their financial decision-making skills are the *payback* method and *rate of return on investment* (Knowler, 1969).

The payback method simply figures how much time it will take a business to pay back expenditures. For example, you purchase $8,000 worth of free weights. You figure you can pay $3,000 a year to the free weight manufacturers in attempting to pay off the equipment. With the payback method you divide the cost of the free weights by the payment per year and you find it will take you 2.67 years to pay off the equipment.

If you take the same $8,000 free weight purchase and estimate the usage by members in your health club, you will net an income of $1,000 per year, and the rate of return or profit percentage derived from this purchase will be 12.5 percent per year. The rate of return on investment is simply calculated by dividing $8,000 by $1,000. Anything at a 12 to 15 percent level is acceptable. Any figure above 15 percent translates into higher business profit levels. Interest on loans or purchases must also be calculated into your rate of return.

Preliminary Control of Finances

This precontrol measure focuses on the budgeting process. Budgets are your planned expenditures for the upcoming year or business cycle. First-level managers are required yearly to submit program and operating budgets to upper management. Most segments of the industry develop what is commonly known as "line-item" budgets. Simply stated, line-item budgeting takes a specific item (i.e., weight machine), gives a brief description of the item and the actual cost. Wise managers will also provide a benefit column which explains the benefit to clientele, employees, and upper management.

Concurrent Control Techniques

Concurrent control techniques involve monitoring day-to-day operations in the workplace and are typically the responsibility of first-level managers (Steinmetz & Todd, 1983). However, it is strongly recommended that middle and upper managers stay in touch with all of the company's employees and that many successful managers practice "open door" policies. Employees should always feel that management is approachable and willing to listen to suggestions or conflicts they might experience on the job.

Concurrent control relies on a variety of techniques: critical incidence reports, 5–15 reporting systems, weekly employee meetings, and daily monitoring of floor operations. *Critical incident reports,* filed by direct managers, are simply short statements, documented by the time and day events occurred. They highlight positive and negative performances by employees. The supervisor uses the critical incident method to verify employee performance in yearly evaluation sessions. The statements are to be placed in the employee's file and assist in decisions to promote or discharge personnel.

The *5–15 reporting* technique takes 15 minutes to write by employees and five minutes to read by employers, hence the name "5–15." It is a terrific opportunity for employees to voice their feelings about their work environment in weekly statements summarizing their impressions about their job, department, and overall working conditions. This alerts the manager to job conflicts and employees' subsequent job satisfaction.

CAUTION: This technique requires time; apathetic and lazy managers *beware!*

Weekly and monthly meetings with employees are only as effective as you make them. All meetings should be justified and complete with agendas. Meetings of this type discuss a variety of topics ranging from employee job training to work stoppages, or even special events at the workplace.

Finally, *monitoring floor operations* calls for what most refer to as "loose-tight" control techniques. Employees don't want to feel as if the manager is monitoring their every move (i.e., Holly Beth case scenario).

Conversely, they also don't want to feel like the manager doesn't care about them. Knowing employees on a first name basis and taking time to know them both on a personal level, as well as professionally, will further assist your ability to monitor daily work performance.

Feedback Control Techniques

This is the final loop in the control area for sport managers (Foster, 1978). Simply stated, **feedback control** examines the actual performance outcomes of employees, financial statements, quality control measures, and management audits. If you remember our discussion of preliminary control techniques, managers must initially control human, material, capital, and budgets. Feedback control assures these initial preliminary control techniques are effectively carried out.

Performance Appraisal

Assessing performance of employees is the least liked control function that managers perform because no one likes to be critical of others' performance and run the risk of being disliked. However, when performed in an objective and fair manner, performance evaluation can be viewed by management and employees alike as a positive experience and an opportunity for all parties to improve performance levels.

All employee appraisals should contain objective and subjective statements, positive comments, areas indicated for improvement, and two-way feedback capabilities. Objectivity typically comes in the form of likert rating scales and a description of the specific performance. Along with an objective rating, management comments should detail the rationale for the rating or a subjective explanation.

Attempting a balance of areas for improvement and positive feedback is highly recommended. The use of stroking phrases such as "we know you are capable of this type of performance" as opposed to "you need to improve your job performance in this area" goes much further with employees. Managers must remember their job is to facilitate and nurture employee growth and development, not tear it down (Amend, 1985).

Remember, evaluations should be a two-way street. Employees should have the opportunity to evaluate their direct supervisor or manager. You, as a manager, must also be willing to learn from employees and improve your performance. Some examples of performance appraisal methods are provided in table 6.2.

TABLE 6.2 Sample Employee Appraisal Statements

Sample A: Likert Scale with Subjective Feedback

Area of Performance Accessing Employee Cooperation		Comments
Low High 1 2 3 4 5		George is always friendly and courteous to other employees.

Sample B: Weighted Checklist

Score	Weight	Comments
1–10, low to high	X 20%	Cooperates well with co-workers, superiors, and clientele

Sample C: BARS Method (Behavioral Anchored Rating System)

Highest Performance	Comments
2.00	Is extremely cooperative with employees, management, and clientele. Behavior instills cooperation in others and contributes greatly to a cooperative workplace
1.75	Cooperates very well with employees, management, and clientele
1.5	Is cooperative with employees, management, and clientele

The more specific you can be about desired work performance, the more specific employee feedback becomes and the fairer you are perceived as a manager. Most consider the BARS rating scale to be the most effective method because it points to specific work behaviors required for performance excellence.

Finally, beware of common errors managers commit when rating employees. Knowledge of the following errors may help to prevent them from occurring in your performance appraisal (Dossett, 1981).

Halo effect: Rating an individual high in all work categories simply because they possess a work behavior that you value greatly. For example, because an employee cooperates well with others and you highly value that characteristic, you rate him or her high on other job performance areas.

Recency effect: An employee was recently sick and productivity suffered as a result; therefore you rate his performance all year as lacking based on the most recent performance.

Central tendency: Rating someone all threes on a five-point likert scale. Managers who rate this way are either rushed or hate to take a stand on particular performance criterion.

Harshness/Leniency errors: Giving all ones or all fives to an employee in all categories of their work behavior. Again, like central tendency, the rater is extremely critical or lenient toward employees.

No one can claim that employee evaluation is easy or not time consuming! Taking the time and going the extra mile when evaluating others typically pays off handsomely in subsequent job performance.

Feedback Control of Materials

The most common form of feedback control of materials is measurement of the number of defects your company produced. This measure is typically more important in the consumer segment, i.e., golf, tennis, racquetball manufacturing. Most companies shoot for a defect rate of under 3 percent of total manufactured goods. The Japanese companies are very efficient in production and manufacturing of goods (similar to preliminary control efficiency levels) with rejection level close to .005 percent. Again, high rejection rates point to malfunctions in labor and/or production of parts (Richardson, 1986).

Management Audits

A management audit is careful scrutinization of all phases of a firm's control techniques. Preliminary, concurrent, and feedback control measures are assessed to assure that a firm is operating with maximum efficiency and are typically performed by outside audit companies who are familiar with the unique demands and operations of your company and/or similar companies. Many firms choose to go to outside auditors for their expertise and objectivity when evaluating a company's operating efficiency. They are typically costly, so many firms choose to bring in auditors on a three-year or five-year basis. Management audits are yet another feedback measure that assure the planned results match actual outcomes or results (Augrist, 1988).

Financial Statement

A final feedback control technique is analyzing a firm's income and balance sheets, more commonly known as developing a financial statement. Expenditures, profits, long- and short-term debts are all examined yearly to assure what was preliminarily budgeted matches the year-end assets and liabilities. A financial statement can tell you when you are overinvested, profits are up, inventory is low—and essentially how profitable your sport business is or isn't. Financial statements are typically analyzed by the business' accountant or financial planner. A sample financial statement is provided in Appendix A (Eagan, 1992).

SUMMARY

1. Control is divided into three phases: preliminary, concurrent, and feedback.
2. Preliminary control techniques help monitor capital, materials, personnel selection, and budgeting process.
3. Employee selection is the most critical preliminary control technique. Designing accurate job descriptions, using appropriate advertising avenues, and developing effective interviewing skills help in selecting the right person for the job.
4. Concurrent control techniques daily monitor employees by using 5–15 reporting systems, staff meetings, and critical incident reports.
5. Feedback control techniques include financial statement analysis, quality control, employee appraisal, and management audits.
6. Employee appraisal systems should be objective, subjective, and two-way.
7. A financial statement analysis examines a firm's income and balance statement. It helps to assure that what was initially budgeted was sufficient for operations.

REVIEW QUESTIONS

1. What is meant by Type I and Type II errors in staff selection?
2. What are appropriate percentages when statistically sampling for defects in manufacturing of sporting goods?
3. What is the difference between the payback and rate of return on investment methods when preliminarily controlling for capital?
4. What does "loose-tight" refer to when monitoring day-to-day operations of employees?
5. What are some common errors committed by managers when evaluating employees?
6. Explain the importance of a management audit.
7. Budgets are to ＿＿＿＿＿＿＿＿ control as statistical sampling is to ＿＿＿＿＿＿＿＿ control.
8. Why should employee evaluations be both objective and subjective?

Do you stick with the old or go with the new?

Decision Making Made Easy

■ ■ ■ ■ ■ ■ ■

CASE STUDY
Which Way Do WE Go? Which Way Do We GO!?

John Sloan possessed great business savvy. Many in the insurance industry admired his ability to make keen and gutsy business decisions and his success as Vice President of Government Relations for the Always Got You Covered Insurance Company helped to assure quarterly profits for the corporation. One day, John decided to branch out in his business ventures and try a new entrepreneurial idea he had recently read about in *The Wall Street Journal*. The latest fitness craze, according to experts, was underwater ankle weights, used by former prize fighters in their quest to be the best. Quickly, he phoned a close colleague for advice. Hannah Barbedoes, who coordinated a sport management program at the local university, thought the idea might have some merit and suggested contacting a marketing research firm for advice on feasibility and marketability of the product. She also recommended he examine several existing mail order businesses for a possible distribution channel.

John felt that the idea just couldn't wait. He proposed plans for the manufacturing to begin with a Mexican firm because labor was much less expensive in Mexico and this would improve profit margins. He established a mail order advertising campaign and received some initial capital from some of his close business associates who wanted in on the profits.

One year later the concept went belly-up. There simply wasn't enough consumer demand for underwater ankle weights. John found himself heavily in debt and doubting the credibility of *The Wall Street Journal*.

DISCUSSION QUESTIONS

1. *What decisions could John have made differently regarding the ankle weight manufacturing?*
2. *If John was so successful in the insurance business, why did he fail in the sport management business?*

■ ■ ■ ■ ■ ■ ■

THE DECISION-MAKING PROCESS

As the scarecrow in the *Wizard of Oz* points out, sometimes life presents us with many different roads we can take and making the best decision is difficult, whether it be personally or professionally. Unfortunately, John Sloan found out the hard way. Decisions affect all aspects of a sport manager's work—from planning, organizing, and controlling to leading and motivating employees. What are the keys to success to becoming an effective decision maker? Let's review the decision-making process once again. The decision-making process follows these essential decision-making steps.

1. Ascertain the need to make a decision.
2. Establish decision criterion.
3. Assign weights to your selected criterion.
4. List alternatives you have to choose from with your decision.
5. Select the best alternative.
6. Implement your decision and evaluate its effectiveness.

Let's begin with determining the need to make a decision. If the decision has been made before, past precedence or decision may dictate how you make a current decision. For example, you have given senior citizens membership discounts in the past and if you don't decide in favor of continuing the practice with future senior clients, you might have some very disgruntled customers or even the possibility of a lawsuit or two.

Timing your decision is also a critical factor. Not all decisions require an immediacy to act. Difficult or complex decisions should call for greater caution on your part. Equally important is making sure you have all the facts before you act.

Once you have established the need to make a decision, you must determine the key point that will help you arrive at the right decision. The important criterion or factor critical to that decision is called "decision criterion." Recalling the job search example in the previous chapter, items such as job security, salary, and opportunities for advancement are all critical job decision determinants. We assign weights to these factors according to their relative importance in the decision-making process. If money is important, salary is given the highest weight; if security is important, then that criterion is allocated the highest weight.

Next, you have to explore any or all the alternatives. For example, if decision "a" doesn't work, what about decision "b"? For example, is it best to stay in your present job? Are there other job opportunities? What is the economy like and future job possibilities? It is always a good idea to see as many options as possible and keep your options open until you arrive at your decision.

Selecting the best alternative is sometimes difficult because every decision carries with it a certain amount of uncertainty—unless you made similar decisions before under similar circumstances. Assigning realistic criterion, weights, and examining all your options makes the whole process considerably less painful. If decision "a" doesn't work, you always have decision "b" to choose from. What other items make the process less painful? If you already possess effective decision-making qualities, your job as a decision maker is easier. The following discussion describes qualities for effective decision making.

QUALITIES FOR EFFECTIVE DECISION MAKING

Four qualities or personal characteristics appear to help individuals make effective decisions: *experience, creativity, good judgement,* and *quantitative skills* (Archer, 1985). Let's see why these criteria are so important.

Experience naturally helps. Having made similar types of decisions under similar circumstances definitely is a plus. It also explains why companies look for experienced managers. If you have experienced similar jobs or decisions you are less likely to make the same mistake twice. Hence, someone's job effectiveness is enhanced, saving the company money in costly mistakes an inexperienced manager might make.

Being *creative* also helps you make decisions. Typically, the more creative you are, the more options or angles you can use to approach a problem or decision. For example, seeing the many uses of a racquetball court in a health club. Once installed, the same court can be used for aerobics, volleyball, squash, yoga, or relaxation classes.

Good judgement is another essential quality. Those who possess sound judgement, otherwise known as "common sense," those who are "street smart," consistently make better decisions. Some are born with this quality of "business savvy" and others have to work at it.

Finally, good *quantitative skills* are important. Analyzing market trends, economic trends, consumer indexes or reports help one make more effective business decisions. Marketing research firms often do this kind of work for the unskilled manager, however, always for a fee.

DECISION TYPES

Managers generally make two types of decisions: *programmed* or *nonprogrammed* (Hunsaker, 1981). **Programmed decisions** are more routine in nature and typically have established guidelines to help you carry out your decision. Examples of programmed decisions are racquetball rules, employee regulations, weight equipment standards, or pool safety rules. First-level managers, because of their direct contact with consumers and employees, are typically responsible for making more programmed decisions. Additionally, programmed decisions usually don't require others to participate in the decision-making process because decisions are so "cut-and-dried." You shouldn't need all levels of management to assist you as a first-level manager in carrying out decisions.

Nonprogrammed decisions are more difficult because these types of decisions do not have previous precedence for carrying out decisions. Examples of nonprogrammed decisions come in many types—establishing a new road race, marketing a new style of golf putter, setting up a new, advanced circuit training program at a club, or establishing a new professional football franchise. These types of decisions are typically made by upper and middle management. They are usually more experienced and use this experience to their advantage.

Nonprogrammed decisions also require greater group input. For example, before implementing that new circuit program, you should ask members if they would prefer this type of training program. Also, do your employees know how to supervise this program or do they even want to? Does your accountant feel you have the money to expend here? How successful is this program at other health clubs? Hence, you begin to see the value of group input with nonprogrammed decisions and the importance of involving those who will be directly affected by the impact of your nonprogrammed decision. Table 7.1 further explains programmed and nonprogrammed decisions made by sport managers (King, 1980).

TABLE 7.1 Sport Managers Decision Options

	Management Level	Decision Example
Nonprogrammed Decisions	Upper Management	New products, programs, events, teams
	Middle Management	Rules, regulations
Programmed Decisions	Lower Management	Policies, procedures

EXERCISE: "LOST AT SEA"

Now is your chance to see how effective your own decision-making skills are! The following Lost-at-Sea exercise lets you decide what you and others consider important survival items if shipwrecked at sea. Pay close attention to the value of group decision making in a nonprogrammed decision-making situation. Read through the directions and complete the exercise, then compare your individual and group responses to the accurate responses by the Maritime Naval Academy. Good luck!

Lost-At-Sea Decision Making

Purpose

The purpose of this exercise is to offer you the opportunity to compare individual versus group decision making.

The Exercise in Class

You are adrift on a private yacht in the South Pacific. As a consequence of a fire of unknown origin, much of the yacht and its contents have been destroyed. The yacht is now slowly sinking. Your location is unclear because of the destruction of critical navigational equipment and because you and the crew were distracted trying to bring the fire under control. Your best estimate is that you are approximately one thousand miles south-southwest of the nearest land.

Lost-At-Sea Decision Making
(*continued*)

Below is a list of 15 items that are intact and undamaged after the fire. In addition to these articles, you have a serviceable rubber life raft with oars, large enough to carry yourself, the crew, and all the items listed here. The total contents of all survivors' pockets are a package of cigarettes, several books of matches, and five one-dollar bills.

	(1) Individual Ranking	*(2)* Group Ranking	*(3)* Ranking Key
Sextant	____	____	____
Shaving mirror	____	____	____
Five-gallon can of water	____	____	____
Mosquito netting	____	____	____
One case of U.S. Army C rations	____	____	____
Maps of the Pacific Ocean	____	____	____
Seat Cushion (flotation device approved by the Coast Guard)	____	____	____
Two-gallon can of oil/gas mixture	____	____	____
Small transistor radio	____	____	____
Shark repellent	____	____	____
Twenty square feet of opaque plastic	____	____	____
One quart of 160-proof Puerto Rican rum	____	____	____
Fifteen feet of nylon rope	____	____	____
Two boxes of chocolate bars	____	____	____
Fishing kit	____	____	____

1. Working independently and without discussing the problem or the merits of any of the items, your task is to rank the 15 items in terms of their importance to your survival. Under column 1, headed "Individual Ranking," place the number **1** by the most important item, the number **2** by the second most important, and so on through number **15**, the least important. When you are through, *do not discuss* the problem or rankings of items with anyone.

Lost-At-Sea Decision Making
(continued)

2. Your instructor will establish teams of four to six students. The task for your team is to rank the 15 items, according to the group's consensus, on order of importance to your survival. Do not vote or average team members' rankings; try to reach agreement on each item. Base your decision on knowledge, logic, or the experiences of group members. Try to avoid basing the decision on personal preference. Enter the group's ranking in column 2, "Group Ranking." This process should take between 20 and 30 minutes, or as the instructor requires.

3. When everyone is through, see Appendix B in the back of the text for the correct ranking, provided by officers of the U.S. Merchant Marines. Enter the correct ranks in column 3, headed "Ranking Key."

4. Compute the accuracy of your individual ranking. For each item, use the absolute value (ignore plus and minus signs) of the difference between column 1 and column 3. Add up these absolute values to get your *Individual Accuracy Index*. Enter it here: _____ .

5. Perform the same operation as in Step 4, but use columns 2 and 3 for your group ranking. Adding up the absolute values yields your *Group Accuracy Index*. Enter it here: _____ .

6. Compute the *average* of your group's Individual Accuracy Indexes. Do this by adding up each member's Individual Accuracy Index and dividing the result by the number of group members. Enter it here: _____ .

7. Identify the *lowest* Individual Accuracy Index in your group. This is the most correct ranking in your group. Enter it here: _____ .

The Learning Message

This exercise is designed to let you experience group decision making. Think about how discussion, reflection, and the exchange of opinions influenced your final decision.

Reprinted from: J. E. Jones and J. W. Pfeiffer (eds.), *The 1975 Annual Handbook for Group Facilitators,* San Diego, CA: Pfeiffer & Company, 1975. Used with permission.

SUMMARY

1. Decision making impacts all aspects of work that a sport manager performs.
2. The decision-making process is a six-step procedure.
3. There are two decision types: programmed and nonprogrammed.
4. Programmed decisions have established guidelines and are made more by lower management.
5. Nonprogrammed decisions lack established decision criteria. These decisions are made more frequently by middle and upper managers and require more group input.
6. Qualities for effective decision making include: experience, creativity, good judgement, and quantitative skills.

REVIEW QUESTIONS

1. How is decision making similar to management-by-objectives (MBO)?
2. Why are sport entrepreneurs effective decision makers?
3. Why is creativity important in decision making?
4. What steps in the decision-making process help to make decision making easier?
5. Cite some examples of programmed decisions made by sport managers. Nonprogrammed examples?
6. Why should you involve others when making nonprogrammed decisions?

Managing People

The following chapters in Part III deal with a final sport management task category, managing people. Most experts agree the single most important ingredient to successful management operations are the people who operate behind the scenes, namely, the employees. They are responsible for pleasing your club members, manufacturing the perfect tennis ball, or assuring that your spectators are well taken care of at sporting events. They can make or BREAK your bottom line profit potential. So how do you make employees happy and productive? The following chapters on motivation, communication, and leadership will show you how!

8

Creating and Maintaining Motivation

■ ■ ■ ■ ■ ■ ■

CASE STUDY
The Fitness Manager and Motivation

You are the new manager at a local fitness facility. Upon arriving on the job, you find that the current aerobic fitness instructor and the racquet sport instructor exhibit directly opposite job personalities. The racquet sports instructor is a quiet, somewhat emotionless individual who primarily keeps a low profile at work. The aerobics instructor is outgoing and "high-strung," completely opposite of the racquet sports instructor. The most concrete observation you make is that the number of members involved in the facility's racquet sports program continues to grow, despite the obvious decline of the popularity of racquet sports across the United States. And even though aerobics participation continues to grow nationally, the fitness instructor who teaches most of the aerobics classes at the club is having trouble filling the classes.

You are baffled. The output does not match the personality types of your program directors. Based on your previous management experience, you had concluded that outgoing personalities are highly motivated and, hence, very productive, and that the reverse is true of introverted personality types. You begin to revise your human behavior assessment techniques and the subsequent relationship to motivation and productivity.

DISCUSSION QUESTIONS

1. *Based on this case, what can you surmise about outward human behavior and its relationship to motivation?*
2. *What does this case tell you about motivation and productivity?*

■ ■ ■ ■ ■ ■ ■

MOTIVATION DEFINED

There are a variety of explanations outlining the basic premise underlying motivation and human behavior. The fitness facility scenario points out how intangible human motivation can be. Definitions such as "exerting greater effort" than those not motivated and "a willingness to do something" do not really pinpoint the true nature of motivation (Steers & Porter, 1982).

The most definitive statement on motivation, provided by Herzberg (1989), will be used as a basis for our motivation discussion. They claim that "motivation is a personality trait that directs intensity and initiates behavior; it cannot be observed, only inferred." Though **motivation** is an illusive trait, the lack of motivation by workers or the inability of managers to develop motivation in their employees often makes or breaks the successful organization.

Based on this definition, how does one successfully motivate his or her employees or oneself toward achieving a goal and exerting greater work effort? A discussion of the motivation process and accompanying motivational theories may provide some answers. This chapter puts the various components of motivation into proper perspective for the reader. Motivation is the focus of this chapter because it is important to the sport manager for several reasons. To begin with, sport managers must understand motivation to assist in increasing their own productivity. Secondly, sport managers must be able to motivate employees to achieve greater work levels. Finally, motivation is contagious. If clientele take notice of enthusiastic and highly motivated staff and management, they, too, get excited about their participation or involvement with the sport organization.

The remainder of this chapter will discuss the motivation process, selected theories that have been used successfully by sport managers in the past, and some special topics in motivation.

THE MOTIVATION PROCESS

Take one moment to test yourself. Was there one goal or pursuit that you really wanted to achieve? What were the particular steps you followed to assist you in accomplishing your goal? Figure 8.1 helps explain the motivation process (Berman, 1985). As you can see, the motivation process is closely linked to goal-directed behavior. Initially, there is an unsatisfied need or goal that one wants to achieve. Secondly, there is the goal-directed behavior and the goal is either satisfied or not satisfied.

There are two extreme behaviors often observed in the motivation process. If the goal is satisfied, the highly motivated individual will continue pursuit of another goal, never really quite satisfied with his/her performance. Often, these individuals remain in a state of continual unsatisfied need which can eventually lead to job burnout. In cases of the other extreme, there are individuals who seldom accomplish goals because of a

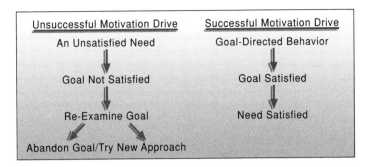

FIGURE 8.1
The motivation process.

failure to adopt a goal-directed behavior pattern. The key to becoming a successfully motivated individual lies in combining the planning and goal-setting skills elaborated on in the management-by-objectives process discussed in chapter 4. Using a prioritized goal system for goal management, there will be less chance of job burnout and a positive means of motivating employees in the work setting. There are several explanations or theories that will assist in your understanding of the motivation process provided in the following sections.

MOTIVATION THEORIES

The following theories have been popularized by individuals in the field of psychology and general management. They are introduced in chronological order—from earliest developed to the most recent. Following the discussion, case studies will assist you in applying what you have learned. It is important that you understand the basis of motivation theory because each subsequent theory contribution provides key elements of dealing with this extremely critical human element—how to get and stay motivated!

Maslow's Needs Hierarchy

Perhaps one of the most cited and discussed theories of motivation was detailed by Abraham Maslow in the late 1930s. As can be seen in figure 8.2, Maslow outlined five levels of human needs in order of importance. These levels are: physiological needs (primary biological needs), safety needs (shelter, safety from physical harm); social needs (love, affection); self-esteem (recognition by peers, family); and self-actualization (becoming totally fulfilled in all areas of human growth and potential) (Maslow, 1970).

FIGURE 8.2
Maslow's hierarchy of
needs.

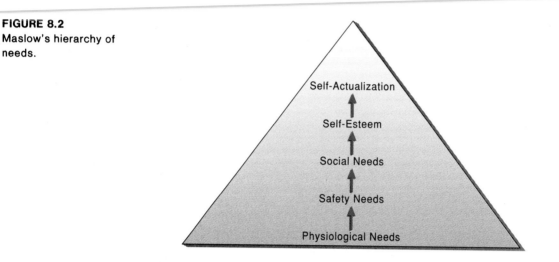

In assessing Maslow's pyramid or hierarchy of needs, one sees that it is easy to comprehend and to apply it to the various stages of motivational development. However, it is Maslow's contention that each of the stages is built upon the next; thus, it is impossible to move on to the next stage without first fulfilling the needs at previous stages. Maslow is frequently criticized for this motivation explanation. Researchers have found that individuals do vacillate from stage to stage at various times in their careers. Another criticism of Maslow's theory is that not every employee has the desire and/or capacity to be driven toward the self-esteem stage or self-actualization stage as a result of his or her job experiences. Some individuals can fulfill these needs through experiences outside the job environment. In 1980, Sergiovanni made an interesting alteration in Maslow's model by adding a self-autonomy stage between the self-actualization and self-esteem stages. He believes this self-autonomy stage exemplifies the worker's need for greater control. Sergiovanni also believes that Maslow's lower order needs (physiological needs) are satisfied more through external rewards and the higher order needs are satisfied more through internal satisfaction. Maslow's theory of motivation is still debated today by motivation theorists. However, his theory helps to understand the first step in the motivation process which is needs clarification (as explained in figure 8.2).

Test yourself. Which of Maslow's levels have you achieved? Which do you hope to achieve?

McClelland's Achievement, Affiliation, and Power Motives

McClelland's motivation theory and its application to the field's sectors of sport management has already been discussed as a component of the involved profit model. It would be remiss, however, not to provide an overview of his theory and its application to the work environment in sport management. The following discussion elaborates on this theory in the workplace.

McClelland proposed that there are three primary motivators in the workplace: achievement, affiliation, and power (McClelland, 1984). Some individuals, according to McClelland, have a compelling drive to succeed for the sake of success alone. These high achievers differentiate themselves from others by their desire to do things better. They seek solutions to problems where they can receive rapid feedback on their performance and where they can set moderately challenging goals. High achievers dislike succeeding by chance; they like to keep score and are very competitive by nature. Most importantly, they tend to avoid very difficult or very easy tasks. Characteristics of high achievers are very closely aligned with those attributes of modern-day entrepreneurs. As a result, many achievers are attracted to the small business management found typically in health and multipurpose clubs (Flamholtz, 1987). The need for affiliation and power is most often found in present-day managers and management success. McClelland's research points out that the best managers rate high in their need for power and low in their need for affiliation.

Most of the attention to McClelland's theory has been focused on the achievement segment. Since the achievement attributes can be taught and have been positively related to higher work performance, sport managers can consider having employees undergo achievement training to improve their performance. Additionally, understanding achievement characteristics and individuals who rank high in this behavior will assist sport managers in explaining and predicting employee behavior.

Herzberg's Motivation Theory

Herzberg's two-factor theory proposes that there are two types of factors pertinent to employee motivation—**maintenance factors** and **motivational factors.** Employees are dissatisfied when *maintenance factors* or "dissatisfactors" are absent from the work environment but don't strongly motivate when present (Herzberg, 1966). These factors that are essential to maintain an adequate level of employee satisfaction suggested by Herzberg are: salary; job security; status; work conditions; satisfying interpersonal relationships with peers, subordinates, and supervisors; technical supervision; company policy; and administration.

Conversely, *motivational factors* called "satisfiers" are conditions that help to motivate employees when present in the workplace but don't result in job dissatisfaction when absent. These satisfiers include: achievement, recognition, advancement, responsibility, possibility of personal growth, and the work itself. Maintenance factors are external to the job itself, whereas motivational factors are tied more directly to the job.

When examining Herzberg's motivational scheme, his ideas share similarities with Sergiovanni's and Maslow's motivational concepts. As Sergiovanni pointed out, Herzberg's maintenance factors or Maslow's lower order needs are satisfied externally to the job. However, motivational factors or higher order needs are tied more closely to the job-centered factors in the workplace. Herzberg's theory is not without criticism. Some critics of Herzberg's theory maintain he utilized too small a sample in his investigation. Also, some believe that the theory may oversimplify the motivation-dissatisfaction relationships and the true sources of job satisfaction and dissatisfaction (McGregor, 1970).

Sport managers can readily apply Maslow's, Sergiovanni's, and Herzberg's ideas to the workplace. The perceptive manager can design jobs that allow for greater task depth and scope by employees, as discussed in chapter 5, which dealt with the organizing function. Also, by using such organizational concepts as delegating authority and decentralization when designing the work environment, greater autonomy, self-esteem, and self-control can be used to motivate employees in the workplace.

Expectancy Theory

Although the early motivation theories offer insight into motivation, none offer a valid model for explaining an individual's drives. What is needed is an integrative model that considers such important elements as individual needs, job design, ability of the employee, and what each job situation might require. The expectancy theory considers all of these factors and the most accurate explanation of what facts drive motivational behavior (Vroom, 1984).

The expectancy theory argues that the strength of a tendency to act in a certain way depends on the strength that the expectation will be followed by a given outcome and on the attractiveness of that outcome to the

FIGURE 8.3
Expectancy model.

individual. It consists of three variables: attractiveness, performance-reward linkages, and effort-performance linkage. According to the expectancy approach, the desire to produce at any given time or situation depends on an individual's goals and the possibility that their individual performance will allow them to attain these goals. Figure 8.3 outlines the expectancy theory.

The strength of one's motivation to perform (effort) depends on the strength of the belief that one will achieve what is attempted. If he achieves this goal (performance), will he be adequately rewarded? If she is rewarded by the organization, will the reward satisfy her individual goals? Generally, the higher these variables, the greater the individual's motivation and the resulting work effort. Sport managers can impact employee motivation by hiring people with the necessary job skills and by providing training and leadership. They can influence performance by being supportive and realistic, and by offering advice. They can influence individual needs by acknowledging employees' special needs and differences.

The theory is readily applicable to the work environment and adds insight into choices, expectancy, and preferences. However, the ideas expressed in the expectancy theory are by far the most difficult to measure (Jordan, 1986).

SPECIAL TOPICS IN MOTIVATION

There are a number of topics within the subject of motivation that have attracted academicians and practitioners in the field of sport management. Three of these topics that deserve special mention here are *equity, money,* and *employee motivation differences in the public and private sectors.*

Equity

It's no surprise to learn of individuals in the sport industry who make more than one million dollars per year and yet are dissatisfied with their job and salary. Since the early 1970s professional athletes' salaries have continued to escalate—yet we still hear of complaints of "low salaries." In baseball, for example, as quickly as some players were signing a long-term contract, others were trying to "renegotiate" their current contract. In 1976 a five-year contract for one million dollars was a prize package. However, by 1978 Reggie Jackson had signed for three million per year and baseball players were suddenly unhappy with what was previously considered by many to be a very substantial income. Recently, Boston Red Sox pitcher Roger Clemens signed a 7.5-million-dollar, three-year contract with the Red Sox organization. Orel Hershiser, determined to show his equivalent dollar value, signed a 7.9-million-dollar contract with the Los Angeles Dodgers. This type of rapid salary escalation presents several questions. What should the elite baseball athlete receive? Upon what is a proper salary based? His teammates? Other players on the baseball team? Other professional athletes? Other entertainers? Age? Experience? Now one can understand why lawyers are brought in during contract arbitration sessions to weed out all the many factors associated with contract negotiations (Schroeder, 1988).

The point *equity* raises is that an individual's motivation is not only affected by the absolute rewards given by the organization, but also by one's relative worth to others. In other words, an individual's level of effort is influenced by absolute rewards received and is also importantly influenced by the relative comparisons of one's input/output ratio to that of others. The perception of what someone gets from job situations (output) in relation to what's put into it (input) is compared to the input/output ratio of relevant others. When the ratios match, a state of equality or equity exists. If not, watch out! People begin to think they are not rewarded properly. Sussmann and Vecchio pointed out in 1982 that attempts by individuals to correct inequities include the following behaviors:

- Making unrealistic claims about their own productivity levels, as well as others'.
- Trying to pressure others to change their productivity levels.
- Changing one's own productivity levels.
- Comparing one's work situation with other work situations.
- Quitting one's job and/or leaving the field.

Equity implications for you as a future manager are clear. In addition to absolute rewards, relative rewards are also critical to satisfying employees and motivating job performance. If an employee envisions inequities in the reward and performance linkage, i.e., if both employees are paid the same, but one is more productive than the other, tension in the workplace could result. Employee awareness of inequity can result in lower productivity, more absenteeism, or an increase in job turnover. With turnover levels close to sixty percent in the health club industry, it is important that those entering that field or related fields be cognizant of equity issues.

Does Money Motivate?

This may sound like a ridiculous question. However, the answer to this question, that yes, money does motivate, must be further clarified. In most instances, *money* is a definite motivational factor, particularly "when you don't have any." One must be cautious about making broad, sweeping generalizations. The following discussion helps to explain the money dilemma.

To some, money is not a motivating factor. However, others are continually driven by the desire to acquire more of it, regardless of how much money they already have. Research indicates that for some, money can be instrumental in satisfying esteem and recognition needs as well as basic physiological needs (Sims, 1980).

If money is to act as a motivator, it is necessary to assume a relationship between performance and rewards. Those who seek money will be motivated to higher performance only if they can clearly *link* high performance to their rewards of more money. Consistent with the expectancy theory, money motivates higher performance only to the extent that money is seen as being able to satisfy the individual's personal goals and is perceived as being dependent upon performance criteria.

Are Public Sector Employees Motivated Differently Than Private Employees?

It is frequently claimed that productivity of public employees seriously lags behind that of employees in private enterprises. One reason frequently cited is that public *employee motivation* is low. But is this true? The following investigation might shed some light on this dilemma.

A study comparing employees in city government organizations with employees in five diverse business firms disproves the stereotype of public employees as security-oriented (Stein, 1982). The findings showed that security was perceived as less important for public employees who had generally greater concern for self-actualization than for employees in the business sample. While the researchers acknowledge that the reduced need for security by public employees, may be, perhaps, because they already possess it, they concluded that public employees viewed self-actualization as a more potent motivating factor than did their counterparts in business. They also showed that public employees were significantly more satisfied with direct economic benefits than private employees.

SUMMARY

1. Motivation can be described as a goal-directed behavior process.
2. Maslow first described motivation as a five-stage process of human development.
3. McClelland theorized that motivation involved achievement, affiliation, and power.
4. Herzberg's two-factor theory described job maintenance and motivation factors, both necessary for job satisfaction of employees.
5. Expectancy theory claims that employees expectations must be met and rewarded for motivation to take place in the workplace.
6. Special issues in motivation include equity, money, and differences between public and private employees.

REVIEW QUESTIONS

1. Why was Maslow's theory flawed?
2. What are higher order and lower order needs?
3. How did the involved profit model incorporate McClelland's motivation theory?
4. Do Herzberg's satisfiers motivate employees? Why or why not?
5. Why is expectancy the most valid explanation of employee motivation?
6. Does money motivate?
7. What occurs when there are inequities in the workplace?

Communicating with IMPACT!

■ ■ ■ ■ ■ ■ ■

CASE STUDY
Why Weight Health Club

Linda Potter prided herself on her ability to talk at length on just about any topic. Linda claimed it was her responsibility to spread the wealth of information she had collected over her three years as manager of Why Weight Health Club. Most of her employees knew that she just loved to talk and seldom paid attention during her management briefings. Everyone just went about doing their daily jobs regardless of what Linda told them. Most of them had experience in the health club industry and felt they could do their jobs regardless how Linda managed. Recently, however, events at the club changed dramatically.

Linda, addressing the employees at their regular monthly meeting, had rattled on at least forty-five minutes over the scheduled meeting time and had totally lost the attention of all the employees, who were either doodling on scratch pads, visiting with other employees, daydreaming, or enjoying a quick catnap before returning to work. She finished her usual speech with an announcement of the new shorter summer hours and subsequent hourly reductions in employee schedules. Much to her surprise, none of the employees had anything to say about the schedule changes. Everyone simply got up and went

back to business as usual. The first day of the summer session arrived with some unusual occurrences.

All the program directors arrived at the usual opening time only to find the club closed and a line of members outside, disgusted with the lateness of the opening. The plumber and electrician, who were to start some repairs an hour earlier, were also waiting outside but no one was there to let them in. The members and workers were baffled because it just wasn't like Linda to be late or miss a day. Someone finally called Linda at home to find out what had happened. Linda was livid when she learned no one knew about the reduction in summer hours. After all, she had told them all at the last meeting and thought all the management surely had informed other employees and members. When Linda finally arrived at the club, many of the members had registered complaints and several employees were threatening to quit because of the reduction in hours— how could they pay their rent or bills? Finally, the club owner, also unaware of the reductions, was furious and waiting for an explanation about the current state of affairs.

For the first time in her life, Linda was speechless!

DISCUSSION QUESTIONS

1. *How did Linda fail in her communication attempts with Why Weight's employees?*
2. *What suggestion do you have for Linda or her employees to assist in improving communication channels at the club?*
3. *Who also should have been informed about the schedule changes other than employees?*

Linda Potter's experience is not uncommon to managers who are inadequate communicators. As Linda found out the hard way, one skill you don't want to leave unpolished as a manager is how to communicate with your many constituents and employees. Why is it so important? This chapter will tell you why!

COMMUNICATION DEFINED

Communication is any form of human expression—written, verbal, or even "body language." It is, for instance, how you express ideas to your employees, send supply requests to your ball manufacturers, or deal with disgruntled members. A definition of the communication process is portrayed in figure 9.1 (Dunham, 1984).

As this figure demonstrates, the cycle begins with an established need to communicate. Linda needed to communicate the new summer hours to employees, formulate a message, and make the announcement at the employee meeting. However, the message never reached the audience to which it was directed and Linda failed to make sure all the employees understood the communication. When she saw the indifferent looks on the part of the employees, she should have asked if they understood the schedule changes. Instead, Linda assumed they knew what she was talking about. She should have even gone one step further—otherwise known as the feedback loop—to remind employees, members, and anyone else affected by the new summer schedule of the change before the schedule went into effect.

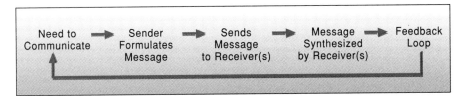

FIGURE 9.1
Communication
process.

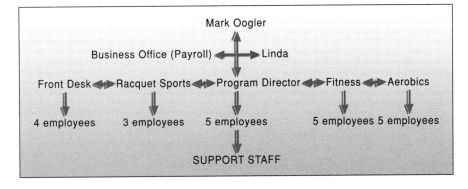

FIGURE 9.2
Vertical communication
channels.

COMMUNICATION CHANNELS IN MANAGEMENT SPORT SETTINGS

There are three pathways or channels that typify most sport businesses: *vertical* communication flow, *horizontal* communication flow, or *diagonal* communication flow (Bacharack & Aiken, 1987). *Vertical channels* parallel the hierarchical chain of command in sport settings. For example, Linda communicates to other program managers about the new schedule changes. Conversely, the program directors communicate back to Linda their feelings about the changes. Figure 9.2 helps to pictorially explain vertical communication (Goldhaber, 1983).

The *horizontal communication channel* is also an avenue for communication flow in a business. For example, the program directors would have made more of an impact in the decision over reduced summer hours if they had discussed the issue among themselves (horizontally) first and then communicated their suggestions to Linda or to their employees and staff (see figure 9.2). However, as the case points out, they never quite got the message in time.

A final channel for communication flow in organizations is *diagonal.* In the case of the Why Weight Health Club, if the business office had also been informed of the new summer schedule, they could have called the electrician and plumber to reschedule their repairs. Payroll also could have informed employees of reductions in pay. All of these efforts would further communicate Linda's message and avoid membership and employee conflicts. Refer to figure 9.2 to observe diagonal communication avenues.

COMMUNICATION STYLES EXAMINED

Table 9.1 outlines four typical communication styles found in the workplace (Hall, 1973). The four communication styles a manager might use are: *arena, unknown, facade,* and *blindspot.* The best communication style is the *arena,* so named because this style resembles an open forum of communication. You and those around you talk freely and openly about ideas, problems, and solutions, creating a very healthy communication environment. Mistrust or conflict in a business is avoided because information is not kept from anyone.

Managers using the *unknown* style have definite communication problems! They don't know how others are communicating around them and others don't understand communication from the manager. There is chaos because no one is communicating to anyone. With this style, both management and those who are communicated to must re-establish lines of communication.

The *facade* was best portrayed in the Linda Potter case study. Linda knew what she wanted to communicate and failed to communicate her message. This caused employees and management to doubt and mistrust Linda's ability as a manager.

The *blindspot* occurs when individuals other than yourself know the communication. It resembles the "best-kept secret" scenario. People are concealing information from you. The following section on dysfunctions and improving communication will give you some ideas on how to deal with the unknown, blindspot, and facade communication breakdowns.

TABLE 9.1 Communication Styles Common to Sport Management

	Settings	
	Unknown to Others	**Known to Others**
Unknown to Self	Unknown	Blindspot
Known to Self	Facade	Arena

COMMUNICATION MISHAPS

As table 9.1 points out, there is only one desirable communication style sport managers should use. How do managers fall prey to the three other communication styles? They develop one or more of the following problems in communication:

- IGNORING THE FEEDBACK LOOP. This problem is a failure on the part of the sender or receiver to follow up on communications. If receivers are unsure of the correct interpretation of information sent, they too should recheck information sent from the sender to assure the message was understood.
- GENERALIZING OR STEREOTYPING YOUR AUDIENCE. Frequently, individuals will make generalizations about others, for example, allowing sex, race, or religion to influence their perception and bias their communication efforts, or failing to accept individual differences in communication and modifying their communications accordingly.
- FALSIFYING INFORMATION. Using "false advertising," some manufacturing companies will advertise free goods or discounted prices. When you read the small print you discover that you really don't receive the discount they advertised. Deceptive business practices can be reported to the Better Business Bureau. This has helped to regulate false advertising attempts by sport businesses.

- SELECTIVE PERCEPTION. With **selective perception,** environmental and personal experiences cause differences in individual perception. For example, you might see the glass half empty or half full, depending on how optimistic or pessimistic you are. Or you might see an image in a picture where others see nothing but a mass of dots during a psychological test. Our perceptions about life make us all different, and understanding why we perceive things differently from others will help us to understand this communication problem.
- UNDERSTANDING THE CAPABILITIES OF YOUR AUDIENCE. There is a tendency by senders to under- or overestimate the comprehension level of the audience they are addressing. For example, Linda was ignored by employees because she failed to use a direct, concise communication style. Communicators must constantly be aware of the capabilities of the audience they are addressing.

SOLUTIONS TO YOUR COMMUNICATION PROBLEMS

There are no easy solutions to communication problems. Understanding the communication process, avenues of communication, style variations, and problems in communication will help to assure you communicate more effectively and avoid communication mishaps.

Remember, communication calls for mutual sharing of information. Provide employees with equal communication opportunities. Develop effective listening skills, which will help you to communicate better and others will know you are truly interested in what they have to say.

MANAGING CHANGE: A SPECIAL ISSUE IN COMMUNICATION

If there is one issue you predict will impact all sport businesses through the year 2000, what do you think it will be? Stumped? The issue we can predict with any certainty is that CHANGE will occur! Employees will change jobs, the economy will change, fads in the marketplace will change, the price of Super Bowl tickets will change, and on and on. Sport managers

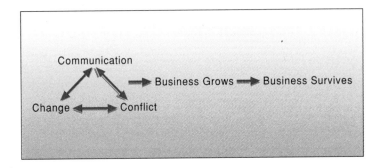

FIGURE 9.3
Managing change.

must understand how best to anticipate, react to, and deal with change as it affects their businesses (Putnam & Pacanowsky, 1983). Figure 9.3 gives you a "change buster" strategy.

When change occurs in a business, it often causes conflict because most people resist change and prefer the "status quo." Because change frequently brings conflict, communication with all affected parties helps to eliminate conflict and bring about change.

Let's return to the Linda Potter example. Linda made a decision to change summer schedules. Recalling chapter 7, this type of decision requires more group input because it is a nonprogrammed decision. Did Linda involve those most affected by change in the decision making? No. Mistake number one. Did she communicate the change to any of the parties affected by the decision? No, she tried and failed to. Mistake number two. How did she deal with conflict as a manager? She didn't; she got upset instead. Mistake number three. Three strikes—you're out.

As you can see, dealing with change is critical to adaptation and subsequent survival in the sport management industry.

SUMMARY

1. Communication can be transmitted verbally, in written form, or with body language.
2. The communication process requires a sender, a need to communicate, a message, receiver(s) of information, and feedback.
3. Organizational communication flow can be vertical, horizontal, or diagonal.

4. Understanding how communication is affected by change and how to deal with subsequent organizational conflict is critical to business survival.
5. There are four communication styles: unknown, facade, blindspot, and arena.
6. Communication problems come in many forms. The most common types include: stereotyping, faulty feedback, falsifying information, selective perception, and capability of the audience.
7. One can become a more effective communicator by empathizing with one's audience and learning to become an effective listener.

REVIEW QUESTIONS

1. We live in an overcommunicated society. Explain this statement.
2. What is the only issue that can be predicted with any certainty through the year 2000?
3. Which communication style calls for more information exposure by others? By self?
4. What communication problem ignores differences in individual perceptions?
5. Explain the ways we can become more effective communicators as sport managers.

How to Best Play the Game
Follow the Leader

■ ■ ■ ■ ■ ■ ■

CASE STUDY
Get the (X?! & % $) out of Dodge!

Harvey Hendricks reflected back on his five years as business manager for the Tucson Tumbleweeds football expansion club with mixed emotions. He was always able to balance the team's budget each year and to Harvey, a clean ledger meant he was an effective manager. However, during his tenure with the organization, many questioned Harvey's business ethics. Employees in the business office were frequently terminated without just cause. Others were promised pay raises that never materialized. He would frequently take days off for his first love, a golf outing, and would treat himself to extended extravagant vacations when employees were seldom afforded such luxuries. He purchased a $300,000 home in the country and drove a new 911 black Porsche which he affectionately referred to as his "little toy."

Harvey began to notice what he considered to be blatant insubordination from his employees, high employee turnover and absenteeism, and productivy at an all-time low. Many of the top executives and the club owner avoided his phone calls and walked the other way when they saw Harvey coming. He became confused and anxious about the organization and his future there— was he paranoid or did people have a lot on their minds? The following week Harvey was called in to the team owner's office and given a two-week notice. The owner cited his lack of good management skills— namely the inability to be a leader to his employees. Harvey was shocked! After all, wasn't the owner pleased he had balanced the budget?

DISCUSSION QUESTIONS

1. *How did Harvey fail to be a good leader?*
2. *What suggestions would you have given Harvey to help avoid the job crisis he experienced?*

■ ■ ■ ■ ■ ■ ■

LEADERSHIP DEFINED

Often considered the most difficult management skill to define, yet the most desired, leadership is the final management function to be mastered in this section on managing people. Leadership requires that sport managers accomplish two things: the ability to influence others and the capability to assume a leadership position. Leadership, like decision making and management-by-objectives, is inextricably intertwined with all the functions a manager performs. To implement plans effectively, you have to lead others. To assure departments are organized efficiently and run effectively, you must possess viable leadership skills. To continually motivate your employees, you have to be a good leader. If leadership is so vital to successful sport management, what makes a good leader? Good followers? Are all leaders managers? Are all managers leaders?

The following sections will help you to answer these questions and provide some insight into the common threads that make up successful leaders (Mintzburg, 1980).

LEADERSHIP THEORIES

Several renowned management theorists have attempted to answer the question, "What makes good leaders?" Their work can be classified into three theoretical categories: *trait, behavior,* and *contingency* theories. These contributions will help us to collectively define leadership and will show us how to best play the management game of follow-the-leader. (Hope you're taking notes, Harvey!)

Trait Theories

C. A. Gibb first posed the question: do all leaders possess similar traits or characteristics that make them more effective leaders? Think for a minute. People in your life you thought were good leaders probably were characteristically charismatic, intelligent, assertive, enthusiastic, empathetic, brave, loyal, and so on. *Trait theorists* believe leaders are born with these traits. The flaw in this theory is that many people who aren't leaders also possess these characteristics. Take for example, Harvey, who was intelligent and assertive but still failed to lead others successfully. Though it doesn't hurt for leaders to exhibit some or all of these traits, the theory doesn't fully explain leadership. Another piece to the puzzle can be found by closely examining behavior theories as detailed in the following paragraphs (Boyatzis, 1982).

Behavioral Theories

Ohio State and Michigan University conducted contrasting leadership investigations during the 1940s. These investigations, responding to highly criticized trait theorists, claimed that leaders were not born with, but could be trained for, leadership behavior. Stogdill of Ohio State found in his investigation that successful leaders were those who were both considerate of employees and skilled at organizing and defining jobs and departments.

Conversely, Likert of the University of Michigan studied two criteria also important for effective leadership, employee-oriented leaders and production-oriented leaders. His investigation found employee-oriented leaders to be more effective leaders. Production-oriented leaders were associated with greater job dissatisfaction and reduced productivity.

Both the Michigan University and Ohio State investigations put forth some further insight into defining leadership. They agreed that being considerate of employees was paramount to effective leadership behavior.

A third, more graphic presentation supporting the work of the University of Michigan and Ohio State was introduced in 1964 by Blake and Mouton. Referred to as the "managerial grid," it pinpointed the importance of creating a shared vision among employees by developing mutual goals and respect. The Blake and Mouton investigation found that most successful leaders exhibited these capabilities.

The leadership picture is still not complete. Theorists thus far have not examined the importance of modifying leadership style according to different situations. The following theories help to elaborate on this concept (Davis, 1979).

Contingency Theories

Tannenbaum and Schmidt, in 1958, developed an autocratic-democratic continuum model to help explain situational or **contingency leadership theory.** They found that in the majority of work groups investigated, democratic leaders who elicited feedback and decision making from their employees had more satisfied employees. However, some work groups investigated were also very productive under democratic leadership while others were more productive under autocratic decision-making situations. With the differences in their findings, they concluded there is need for examing the situation and the characteristics of the employees is critical for effective leadership.

House, in his 1971 Path-Goal model, found that a particular task an employee was working on called for variations in leadership styles from management. If a task was routine and structured, for example, the employee enjoyed less input and greater individual control over his or her job. However, if a task was complicated or ambiguous, employees wanted further direction or leadership from management on what was a clear path toward achieving job goals. They concluded as one's job or task varies, so should the type of leadership influence.

A final contingency theory introduced by Buck Rodgers, in his book, *Getting the Best Out of Yourself and Others* (1988), focuses on individual employee leadership needs. If, for example, the employee is less educated, unmotivated, not work-ego centered, dislikes making job-related decisions and is inexperienced, the manager should use a more autocratic leadership style, assuming a greater leadership role. However, if the employee is highly educated and motivated, is very work-ego centered, wants to impact in the decision-making process and is experienced, the manager should exercise a more democratic leadership style. This employee wants to assume a greater leadership role in his job (McClelland & Boyatzis, 1982).

Two management areas should be developed so that you become a successful leader: understanding what the situation calls for and closely examining individual employee needs. If the work task is very complicated but the employee has experience in performing that particular task, allow for more employee freedom and choose a more democratic (participatory) leadership style. On the other hand, let's say the task is routine and less complicated but the employee is new to the job. The situation may call for a more autocratic leadership style.

What makes a good leader? Good followers! Remember the importance of hiring the right person for the job, establishing a shared vision of how to accomplish job goals, and realizing that every situation and employee calls for a reassessment of your leadership style. If you can balance all these job factors you are on your way to successful sport management in the 1990s (Hatakeyama, 1989).

SUMMARY

1. Trait theories believe that leaders are born with certain traits that make them more effective in leadership positions.
2. Behavioral theories claim that leaders can be trained to exhibit certain leadership behaviors such as concern for employees or initiating structure.
3. Contingency theories value the importance of situational analysis. Each situation may call for a different leadership style.
4. Clarifying paths for employees helps in subsequent goal achievement.
5. Individualizing your leadership approach is critical to motivating and leading employees.

REVIEW QUESTIONS

1. Why were the trait theories inadequate in their explanation of what makes a good leader?
2. How did the University of Michigan investigation differ from the Ohio State studies on leadership? How were they similar?
3. What criteria did the managerial grid point out as a key factor in establishing effective leadership behavior?
4. What are the two continuum points that determine situational leadership?
5. What is meant by Path-Goal leadership?
6. What type of employees respond better to autocratic leadership style? To democratic leadership style?
7. Why do good followers help managers lead more effectively?

Special Topics in Sport Management

The following chapters deal with special management issues sport managers use in their day-to-day operations. An awareness of public relations, marketing, legal issues, computer applications, and management ethics assist skills we have discussed in previous chapters.

Preventing legal hassles is a part of the planning process. Computerized membership billing and accounts assists in the budgeting and control process. An awareness of the needs and interests of target markets and publics allows for more effective communication with these publics. These special issues complete the management picture and provide you with a comprehensive understanding of what sport managers really do!

Relating and Responding to the Needs of the Consumer

A Lesson in Profit

■ ■ ■ ■ ■ ■ ■

CASE STUDY
The Jean Hardcore Story—Everything You Didn't Know about Public Relations and Marketing and Were Afraid to Ask!

Ralph had been with Dipsy Doodle Health Kicks Club for nearly six months when the owner/manager came to him with news the club was closing. Jean Hardcore had sunk every penny of her inheritance money into Dipsy Doodle and figured that the only health club in the small town of Rolling Rock, Wyoming would surely be profitable. She had never run a business before but heard from some of her friends that health clubs were a good investment. She had thought, "What the heck, there is no competition for miles—it just has to work." She set about building the glitziest, stylish club possible, with the most elaborate, state-of-the-art facilities and equipment. She hired some young, part-time college-aged students to run the facilities and programs. The club offered all the programs she heard the fancy ones in Southern California offered. She opened the doors in early summer and was enthusiastically waiting for at least one-third of the 5,000 townspeople to join.

Initially, people seemed interested in the club, but when people found out the cost of memberships and the program selection, they never returned. She was able to sell a few memberships to job transfers from the East and West Coast, but that wasn't paying the bills!

Then one evening Jean stopped into her favorite restaurant, The Greasy Spoon. Halfway through her meal, she overheard a conversation and chuckling at a nearby table. She listened as one customer was saying, "Have you heard about the new, fancy, overpriced health club in town? No one likes the looks of it. It's too expensive and doesn't Jeanie know most of us work so hard on our farms and cattle ranches that who has energy to work out? I can't even pronounce the names of the equipment you work out with, and adjusting all those gadgets just to work up a sweat—forget it!" Another women chimed in, "And who ever heard of a health club called Dipsy Doodle—sounds like they named it after one of my cows!" The whole table then burst out laughing.

Jean got up and stormed off, leaving everyone in shock. One month later, Jean filed for bankruptcy and closed the club.

DISCUSSION QUESTIONS

1. *Was Jean in tune with the community's needs and wants?*
2. *Was Rolling Rock a good location for a health spa? Why? Why not?*
3. *What could Jean have done differently to market the club in this community?*
4. *What other types of communities or locations might be more appropriate for this club?*

■ ■ ■ ■ ■ ■ ■

The Jean Hardcore story is still yet another case of what *not* to do! How can one possess great management skills, offer an outstanding sport product, or provide a sport service unmatched by others and still fail? If you fail to understand a consumer's perceptions about a service or product, if you underestimate a consumer's needs, wants, or desires from a product or service, or if you fail to effectively position a product in the mind of the consumer, you limit your ultimate success as a sport manager. Jean had a tremendous facility, and certainly a business monopoly by offering the only club in town, but never bothered to take into account what the various publics or markets who would be joining and utilizing the facility really wanted. Hence, she failed to acquire sufficient members to pay the bills and had to close up shop. The following sections on public relations, marketing, and positioning your product or service will prevent you from making the same mistakes.

PUBLIC RELATIONS DEFINED

What is public relations? Cutlip, Center, and Broom define **public relations** as a group consensus or attitude about an issue or topic. How does a group arrive at a consensus or attitude about an issue? The roots of our attitudes come from a variety of sources, some of which sport managers can directly influence, others they can indirectly influence. Let's examine some of these roots, and their impact on an individual's attitude development.

Childs (1980) first discussed what he called *primary and secondary attitude development factors.* Primary factors are things we see, hear, or experience in the environment around us. Examples of primary experiences include advertising campaigns, newsletters to members or employees, or even what the townspeople of Rolling Rock felt about Dipsy Doodle and/or health clubs in general. Primary factors come in written, verbal, and visual forms of communication.

Secondary factors, not quite as impactful but still important in shaping our attitudes, include: *culture, family, religion, education, age, gender, social and ethnic groups,* and *social economic status.*

Cultural differences help explain why people in the United States prefer football and why the Japanese prefer martial arts (Paisley, 1981).

Family attitudes also impact the formation of our attitude base. Most of us spend at least 18 years of our lives listening to opinions shared by parents and/or siblings. Think of the tremendous impact these people have on our opinion formation.

Religious beliefs also affect moral and ethical stances surrounding a variety of issues.

Ethnicity can affect perceptions and attitudes about life and sport. Role models of a similar ethnic group can provide guidance for the youth of the population segment.

One's social economic status also impacts attitude development. Inner city youths might gain more exposure to basketball, football, or track and field. Suburban youth perhaps gain more exposure to country club or health club programs and sports because their families are more apt to afford these experiences.

Age also impacts attitudes and sports. Individuals over forty might prefer more lifetime sports experiences. College-age individuals may prefer team sports.

Gender can also influence sport selection and opportunities to engage in certain sports—such as football (primarily a men's sport) or field hockey (primarily a women's sport) offered exclusively to males. Also professional sports opportunities are limited to only two sports, tennis and golf. This further limits opportunities for women in sports.

Finally, education and educators assist in our attitude and opinion formation by broadening our cultural, historical, anthropological or sociological knowledge base. For example, students who receive degrees in liberal arts may hold different world views than a student majoring in business.

Social groups we belong to also influence our attitudes. Alumni associations, church groups, or community service groups hold group views or opinions that affect our attitudes.

Variations in Public Relations Settings

Public relations takes on many forms in a variety of settings. In government-related organizations, public relations may be called public affairs. In college and school settings, it might be referred to as the developmental or fund-raising office. In politics, it's referred to as lobbying or acquiring political or public support. Press agents are public relations representatives for entertainers; sport agents are public relations representatives for professional athletes. It must be stressed, however, that every employee associated with a firm or business who comes in contact with the public impacts how the public perceives that business or organization and therefore plays an important public relations role.

Terms Confused with Public Relations

Public relations sometimes becomes confused with other terms such as publicity, advertising, marketing, or positioning. **Publicity** is a nonpaid form of advertising, frequently used by public relations practitioners in the form of news releases or radio (public broadcasting announcements) or television (news coverage). Publicity as a tool requires prior planning but very little funding by organizations, therefore it becomes a popular form of communicating to an organization's various publics (Harlow, 1976).

Advertising, on the other hand are paid forms of announcements, such as advertising in magazines, newspapers, television commercials, billboards, newsletters, brochures, etc.

Marketing differs from public relations in that the aim is to an actual exchange of money for services rendered or products sold. Marketing, for example, tries to sell more tennis shoes in a specific marketplace by identifying needs and wants, and competitors' marketing strategies. Public relations attempts to lay the groundwork or foundation for marketing by swaying publics or targeting markets to develop positive attitudes or opinions about your service or product.

Positioning affects both marketing and public relations strategies for organizations. How you position a product or service in the mind of the consumer depends on their opinion about your organization and what their present needs and wants might be. Positioning is also affected, as with mar-

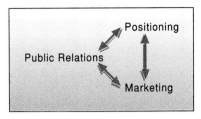

FIGURE 11.1
Public relations, marketing, and positioning.

keting, by competitors' positions and respective positioning strategies. Figure 11.1 helps to pictorially explain the important marketing, public relations, and positioning working relationship.

The Impact of Trends and Fads

Now that we have examined the various components of the public relations definition, we have to explore the importance of trends and fads when establishing effective public relations programs. Fads, not to be confused with trends, start from management and spread downward to the various publics or constituents. They are relatively short lived unless they become established trends. For example, many sport clothing manufacturers deal with faddish styles, with consumers often demanding newer, different clothing designs (Naisbitt, 1982).

Trends, on the other hand, start from the bottom and spread upward. They may last for years and are grounded in public opinion. Societies needs and wants dictate trend development and direction. For example, the fitness trend, originating in the late 1970s has gained strong momentum. An overwhelming majority of the American public realizes that exercise is good for them. The how to and what kind of exercise becomes the challenge for you, the commercial sport manager. State-of-the-industry reports released by almost all of the sport industry segments address national consumer trends yearly. Remember: don't commit the same mistake Jean did!

The Public Relations Process

How does one establish, maintain, or strengthen public relations? The following four-step process helps to diagram the development of a public relations program (see table 11.1).

TABLE 11.1 The Public Relations Process

Step 1: Critically assess the situation
Step 2: Develop a public relations plan
Step 3: Communicate the plan to internal and external publics
Step 4: Evaluate the plan's effectiveness, modify or enhance the existing plan

---

Step 1: Find out what is going on! Describe the current situation by answering the following key questions (Lindenmann, 1980):

- What do people think about your business? Competitors? The industry in general?
- Where geographically are your boundaries for your public relations (PR) plan? 5 miles? 10 miles? Statewide? Nationally?
- Who are your possible customers? Competitors? How do they use information? What types of information do they attend to?

To collect information about the situation, one can use informal methods such as personal contacts, community focus groups, telemarketing surveys, hot lines, etc. Formal methods of information gathering include market research firms, Gallup polls, U.S. Census Bureaus, or specific industry research reports.

Step 2: Next, based on information collected, develop that public relations plan of attack. Your plan should address the following questions:

- What are your program's goals and objectives? Does it build positive public relations? Does it change negative PR?
- Who are your target publics who will be directly affected by your PR plan? Are there specific objectives for each public?
- What are your message and media strategies?
- How and by whom will the plan be evaluated?
- Who will be assigned what responsibilities?
- How much money will it take?
- What is the time frame for releasing information and the plan itself?

Step 3: How will you communicate this plan to both internal and external publics? The following internal and external line of questioning should be undertaken:

Internal Publics:
- Does each employee understand the goals and objectives of the public relations plan?
- Is there candid information flowing in all directions which develops mutual trust between employer and employee? (i.e., newsletters, regular meetings)?
- Do employees feel management will listen and take time for their individual needs?

External Publics:
- What are your external publics like? What are their values, attitudes, demographics, and social economic class?
- Who or what groups impact public opinion the most? Religious, government, community leaders?
- What communication strategies will you use? Open house? Special events? Local television, newspapers, magazines? Volunteer work or community service? Newsletters?

Step 4: How effective/efficient was your public relations effort? Some questions suggested for inclusion in the evaluation process include (Rossi & Freeman, 1982):
- Are you meeting your goals, objectives?
- Are you reaching selected target publics?
- Are the public relations effects positive? Negative?
- Is the plan worth it? Cost effective?
- Are all resources (human and financial) used effectively?

MARKETING DEFINED

Is the sport marketing approach different from any other type of business? What makes marketing sports events different from marketing a toothpaste brand? One can predict with near certainty how consistently a toothpaste will perform. However, it is exceedingly difficult to predict college or professional football team results because of the uncertainty of human behavior and performance.

When 300 college administrators were asked what they thought marketing was, 90 percent responded with "public relations," "advertising," and "promotions." The other 10 percent indicated they thought it was market research, product development, pricing, and promotion. Why the confusion? Many practitioners use the terms interchangeably, casting doubt on the true meaning of marketing.

As already indicated, marketing a product or service should produce an actual exchange of money or transaction. This process differs from public relations, whose major consideration is to modify or enhance public opinion. Marketing's major consideration then is to satisfy human needs, wants, and demands through an exchange process (a transaction) involving services or products.

Recall chapter 8, which dealt with motivation and human need satisfaction. A review of the motivation process and Maslow's theory explaining higher order and lower order needs is warranted at this point. The main consideration for a marketer is to satisfy human needs, wants, and demands. Let's look at these three areas separately (Kotler, 1983).

Understanding human needs: Why some individuals feel certain needs must be satisfied or why one might choose to extinguish a desire for some other need. For example, one might need to work out on a daily basis, but only require a sturdy pair of jogging shoes, an old tee shirt, and shorts (i.e., achievement).

Wants: Different from needs; shaped by an individual's needs and the cultural setting. Jean tried to transplant the East and West Coast wants into Rolling Rock culture—Wrong!

Demands: Focused on purchase power. One might have many wants but can only afford a select few. Once again, the townspeople couldn't afford the membership prices at Dipsy Doodle, hence, no purchase power or demand for the service.

The closer you match the needs, wants, and demands of your target markets and publics, the more they will want to acquire your product or service. The marketing definition would not be complete without a discussion of markets, marketing, marketing management, and societal marketing. **Markets** are actual or potential buyers of your product. **Marketing**

FIGURE 11.2
The marketing
definition.

is the actual activity that takes place during the marketing process, involving telemarketing, selling and/or promoting practices. **Marketing management** is the planning, organizing, and controlling of all marketing procedures, from market research to marketing program evaluation.

For your review, figure 11.2 provides the framework for the marketing definition. Whether marketing a service, product, or idea, the process remains the same. The following section elaborates on the marketing process.

The Marketing Process

The marketing process involves a three-step process: analyzing market opportunities, selecting target markets, developing a market mix—all made effective by sound marketing management procedures (Frank, Massy, & Wind, 1972).

Step 1: Analyzing market opportunities. When analyzing marketplace, ask the following questions:
- Is it difficult to break into the industry? High capital requirements? Superior location?
- Are the competitors weak? Would you hold a competitive advantage?
- Are there fewer or less satisfactory product/service substitutes?
- Does the market opportunity match your company's mission, objectives and available resources (human and financial)?

Step 2: Selecting target markets. This measures market demand, market segmentation, and market targeting.

Measuring market demand, assisted by consumer indexes and rating reports, identifies all competitive services or products sold. It examines future growth potential or what consumer demand will be based on demographic shifts or changes.

Marketing segmentation, based on what your demand tells you, identifies all customers who exhibit need for your product or service (for example, all males and females between the ages of 25 and 45 that exercise regularly).

Market targeting, based on the needs and identified customers, selects the best target market for your product or service. (With Dipsy Doodle, target markets would include those males and females who exercise regularly, who receive incomes of over $35,000 per year, and who have joined health clubs before or express an interest in joining a health club.)

Step 3: The marketing mix or determining price, promotion strategies, product/service strategies, and distribution strategies. Some appropriate questions to assist in developing your marketing mix strategies include the following:

What types of consumers actually use and purchase this product? Other brands?

What strategies can be developed to attract new markets or consumers?

What specific needs or wants are fulfilled through this product/service use?

How much does price affect the purchase power of consumers?

What types of media affect consumer use?

How frequently is this service/product purchased by consumers?

ADVERTISING AND PROMOTION STRATEGIES

Special mention must be made here of specific advertising and promotional strategies available to the sport manager or those who market sport businesses. One major reason most of these businesses fail is because they fail to introduce effective advertising and promotion campaigns. The following discussion addresses key advertising and promotion points that help you to impact target markets with pizazz!! (Blake & Bly, 1983).

Advertising

Advertising includes sponsorship of any paid communication that assists in promoting ideas, product, and/or services. Billions of dollars are spent yearly by private companies and corporations. The most frequent forms of media used in advertising campaigns include: magazines, radio, television, direct

---

TABLE 11.2 Advertising Campaign Components

Objectives:	Which products or services does our company want to develop, invest in, or provide exposure?
	What media do our target markets attend to most?
	How do we want to impact product or service sales?
Cost:	What percent of total product sales do we want?
	What do our competitors spend on advertising?
	Do we have the human and financial resources to be successful?
Message:	What do we want to say?
	How do we want to say it?
	What types of messages do our target markets attend to most and why?
Media:	What are the advantages and disadvantages of the various media types?
	How frequently and what kind of impact do we hope to create?
Evaluation:	How did our message impact target markets?
	How did our advertising affect sales volume?
	Were there any negative or unintended results from our advertising efforts?
Feedback:	How should we modify our advertising campaign in the future?

---

mail, billboards, posters, signs, catalogs, or directories. The many uses of advertising include product or brand advertising, service advertising, institutional advertising, or special event advertising. Table 11.2 summarizes important advertising steps.

Let's elaborate on table 11.2. Advertising objectives normally take on three forms. They hope to inform target markets about something, i.e., a new product, price changes. They might also want to persuade target markets to purchase a new product or service. Finally, they might remind a public about something, an upcoming event or, perhaps, the season opener.

When formulating a message, consumers typically expect four areas of need satisfaction; a *rational reason* for using the product (will run faster), a *sensory gratification* (Gatoraid guarantees to quench that thirst), *social gratification* (membership in our club will help you meet fun people), and *ego gratification* (the tanning booth will make me more desirable). Need gratification will often result from product/service use or take place during product/service use.

Message style is also a critical consideration. Below are the types of styles one can choose, along with some industry specific examples (Kotler, 1983).

- Slice of Life: The family is shown working out in a health club.
- Life-style: Some inner city youths playing a pick-up game of basketball.
- Fantasy: Cruising on the love boat and meeting that special person on board.
- Mood or image: The tennis shoe for the young executive on the run.
- Musical: A high-impact aerobics class commercial performed to music by Madonna.
- Personality symbol: Michael Jordon working out with Nike products.
- Technical expertise: Titleist Golf Division demonstrating the month-long process involved in manufacturing their golf balls.
- Scientific evidence: A Nautilus machine showing scientific evidence that working out with their machine improves muscular strength.
- Testimonial: Quotes from satisfied customers about the quality of experience provided at the local health club.

Media decisions examine media impact on target markets, the frequency with which they might receive information, and the relative impact the media has on the listener. Market research firms can tell prospective advertisers about the key concerns involving appropriate media selection.

The scheduling of advertising is also important. Most experts recommend advertising one month prior to an event or the start of a season, with follow-up advertising one week prior. Many health clubs begin advertising after the first of the year because many individuals choose losing weight as their New Year's resolutions or are concerned about weight gain over the holidays or fitting into that bathing suit in the spring. Carefully examining competitor advertising can help better your advertising position and strategies. Finally, evaluate your advertising campaign. Did it read your target markets? Did it have any ill-intended effects? What would you keep or change for next year's advertising strategies?

Promotions

Promotions help to stimulate market penetration and advertising efforts. Examples of promotional tools that advertising campaigns use include free samples, coupons, price packages, or complimentary gifts. Noting which campaign promotions were used successfully by competitors in the past will also provide some insight into development of your promotional campaign. Size of promotions, conditions, timing, duration, cost, and distribution vehicles are also concerns when developing promotion ideas.

POSITIONING YOUR PRODUCT OR SERVICE

Al Reis and Jack Trout in the mid-eighties added a new marketing dimension they entitled "positioning." This concept stressed the importance of **positioning** a product, service, or idea in the mind of the consumer. Their rationale for using this approach, in addition to marketing to consumer needs, wants, or demands, was that we live in an "overcommunicated" society. Hence, we are constantly bombarded with advertisement and marketing attempts as consumers. The key, according to Reis and Trout, is to try to find a way into the mind of the consumer by going beyond traditional marketing and advertising strategies. Their suggestions are as follows:

> **Suggestion One:** If a product or idea has established leadership in the marketplace it probably resulted from "being there first." Being "firstest with the mostest" is the most effective way to establish leadership. To maintain leadership in the marketplace, it is important to stress value not the fact that you are number one. Reebok's tennis shoe "Pump" is a good example of being "firstest with the mostest." Their strategy is to stress performance over position.

> **Suggestion Two:** If you are not the leader, find the hole left by the leader. Because a leader cannot be all things to all people, Reis and Trout suggest that one look for the *cherchez le creneau* or the markets the leader has not captured. There are many types of holes available that one can use to position his product or service (Reis & Trout, 1986):

>> **Size Creneau:** If competitors emphasize the large size of their health club facility, you could stress the small, intimate, and personal atmosphere of your facility.

Price Creneau: Making price an advantage. Your golf club membership is priced higher for those with "distinctive taste."

Age Creneau: Recreational and retirement communities for aging populations.

Time Creneau: Wheaties—the breakfast "champions" eat to get them going in the morning.

Distribution Creneau: Jack LaLane, first to bring fitness to millions through the medium of television.

Suggestion Three: Importance of the name. A product or service name should be simple and easy to relate to the source. For example, Dipsy Doodle was not an appropriate name to position the club in Rolling Rock. Acronyms are also discouraged unless the name is already so well known and popular, the initials are easier to say or remember, i.e., IBM.

Suggestion Four: Avoid line extension. Avoid naming a product similar to a previous product that was successful, for example, Nautilus II named after a very popular Nautilus I workout machine. Nautilus II will fail to gain recognition on its own merits because of consumer association with Nautilus I.

SUMMARY

1. Public relations paves the way for successful marketing.
2. Positioning helps to assure marketing strategies find their way into the mind of the consumer.
3. Public opinion and attitudes help to make up the framework of public relations.
4. Public relations is critical for business survival in the information age.
5. Public relations is a four-step process: situational analysis, planning, implementing/communication, and evaluation.
6. Internal public relations communication deals with employees inside organizations; external public relations focuses on external publics that interact with a firm.

7. Marketing examines consumer needs, wants, and demands. It implies a service or product is exchanged and targets markets who would best be served by products or services.
8. Market segmentation helps to determine all possible individuals who demonstrate a need, want, and demand for a service.
9. The market mix answers pricing, promotion, place and product/service questions about the product or service you are introducing to the marketplace.
10. Effective advertising must examine objectives, cost, media, message evaluation, and feedback of the campaign.
11. Positioning is impacting the mind of the consumer.

REVIEW QUESTIONS

1. What are some terms often confused with public relations?
2. Explain the difference between primary and secondary attitude factors.
3. Is public relations an attempt to "manipulate" publics' attitudes? Explain.
4. How is marketing different from public relations?
5. How is advertising different from promotions?
6. Explain what is meant by societal marketing.
7. Positioning is what you do to a product or service. Is this statement true or false?
8. If you are not a leader in the marketplace, what other positioning strategies can you pursue to gain market share?
9. Why is a product or service name so important?
10. How is positioning different from marketing?

Staying on the Side of the Law
Preventing Legal Hassles

■ ■ ■ ■ ■ ■ ■

CASE STUDY
The Night the Lights Went Out at the Forum

Joe Shots and Don Fearnone were on their way to the pro hockey season opener at the Forum between the hometown favorite Sharpshooters and the cross-state rival, Riveters. As usual, they stopped off at their favorite sports bar, O'Hardies, to catch the happy hour specials and knock down a few beers. They arrived at the game a couple of minutes late; each ordered a giant size beer, and strolled toward their seats.

As the game went on, it appeared both Joe and Don were quickly becoming inebriated and became agitated over every official's call that went against their team. Pierre Cardonte, the most physical player for the Riveters put a body check on Bob Lafonte, the top player for the Sharpshooters. Don Fearnone was

certain Pierre's move was high sticking. Don, in a drunken craze, jumped the hockey restraining wall and, with his fists swinging wildly, headed toward Pierre. The nearest official, fearing for the safety of the players, skated frantically toward Don, tackling him and sending him flying toward the restraining wall, where he lay unconscious for several minutes.

When Don was revived, his left side was sore and he had a nice bump on his forehead. Paramedics were called and whisked Don off to the nearby hospital. Once there, the doctors examining Don found several broken ribs. Several days later, Don filed suit for battery against the official.

DISCUSSION QUESTIONS

1. *Could this incident have been prevented?*
2. *Was the official wrong in his actions?*
3. *Name all the parties that might be involved in the lawsuit or have reason to countersue.*

■ ■ ■ ■ ■ ■ ■

A POINT OF DEPARTURE

The United States is one of few countries around the world where litigation and lawsuits greatly affect the way we live, what we consume, and especially how we play or participate in sports. This legal trend did not always play such a pervasive part in American society. Until the 1960s no one ever thought of suing the government, a teacher, and definitely not, a coach. The respect for authority figures and institutions was unquestioned by its people.

Paramount change occurred in the 1960s. A growing concern for individual rights, combined with a loss of respect for authority figures and institutions, changed the shape of the legal system. People believed it was their right to sue if their individual freedoms were impinged upon. For these reasons, it is important you understand the way our judicial system operates, legal vehicles that protect individual rights, legal trends in society and sports, and how to prevent lawsuits from occurring. REMEMBER, lawsuits could happen to you as a sport manager, so let's find out how to prevent the situation at the Forum from ever happening to you!

THE JUDICIAL SYSTEM

Where do state and national laws originate and how are they enforced? There are three branches of government both at the state and federal level that provide legal direction for the principles that govern American society. These branches, judicial, legislative, executive, are interacting systems that assure democracy is carried out through a system of "checks and balances." Each branch impacts and serves to regulate the other two branches to prevent dominance by any branch. Figure 12.1 explains this idea of checks and balances.

Reflecting on Figure 12.1, let's say you wanted to eliminate sports gambling nationally. You begin the process by contacting your legislative representatives (senators and representatives) and ask them to develop and support a bill that would make all sports gambling illegal. This law, once passed by the legislature and signed by the President of the United States would become effective and subsequently enforced by federal or state administrative bodies (executive branch). Violators of the law would then be apprehended by executive law enforcement agents (police or FBI), indicted, and forced to stand trial by the judicial branch (judges and prosecutors).

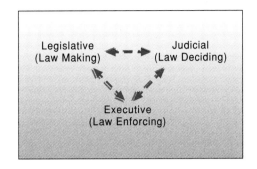

FIGURE 12.1
The branches of
government.

The Court Systems

The judicial system generally decides all cases in a number of ways. The court could require damages (money) from those who violate laws and cause injury to another person or party. They could require someone to complete an obligation (fulfill their part of a contract). They could prevent a disobedience (place a restraining order preventing a group from doing business). Finally, they could punish someone if they break a law (jail term or fine) (Cardozo, 1962).

The courts decide on both private cases (between two parties, e.g., divorce) and public cases (public agency practices, e.g., athletic director fires the football coach at a public high school). Courts in all states, with the exception of Louisiana, decide cases on case law, or on what previous cases have ruled. They cite a case, *Smith* v. *Smith,* for example, as similar to the case that is being tried and use the findings to support their arguments. Louisiana, the only state that requires courts to go by written law, allows for no deviation from the written "letter of the law" and does not permit reference to other previously decided cases.

Distinction between Federal and State Judicial Systems

The first ten amendments to the Constitution are the Bill of Rights. They are the basic "law of the land" and provide the rules, standards, and principles that govern relationships of people in all fifty states. The Bill of Rights had to eventually be modfied to meet the ever changing needs of society. Hence, an additional 26 amendments were added (Round, 1908). Of particular interest to sport managers are the following amendments:

First: Protection of our personal freedoms: speech, religion, press, and assembly (e.g., media covering a professional basketball game)

Fifth: The acquisition of property for public and/or private use (e.g., acquiring property for building a health club); and due process guarantees for all citizens in the United States

Tenth: Any legal responsibility not outlined in the first ten amendments become a state function (e.g., state income tax deducted from employees varies from state to state)

Fourteenth: Due process protection was extended from the fifth amendment to assure that all states protect the rights of their citizens (e.g., if an employee is arrested by XYZ Health Club manager for selling illegal drugs (steroids), they are entitled to their rights to a speedy trial).

Tort Liability

A critical legal area from which the majority of sport-related lawsuits are derived is that of **tort liability.** Tort comes from the Latin term, *torquire,* which means "twisted." The name explains why tort is defined as a legal wrong which results in injury to a person or property. Essentially it implies you "twisted" the law or violated a law that caused injury to others.

Tort law comes from two legal sources, written and common laws. If you recall our discussion earlier, all laws come from these two sources—either from what the legislative branch enacts or case law from the judicial system. Since the majority of states (49) use common law, the remainder of the discussion will focus on common law tort issues. Common law torts that are committed by individuals can be classified as *unintentional* or *intentional.* The following section explains both types.

Unintentional Torts

The most common form of unintentional tort committed by individuals is **negligence.** Negligence is, essentially, a failure by someone to act as a reasonably prudent person would. What does this mean? (Prosser, 1974). There are three factors that must be present for a person to be guilty of negligence:

1. Duty: owing someone to act with reasonable care. (Example: A football coach is responsible for the health and safety of players.)

2. Breach of duty: Not fulfilling your duty to act with reasonable care. (Example: The football coach leaves practice unsupervised to answer a phone call.)
3. Causation: Breach of duty causes a negligent act to occur. (Example: A fight between two players results with one of the players seriously injured.)

If one is accused of negligence, you have several defenses you can use to defend your actions: *assumption of the risk, contributory negligence, comparative negligence,* and *vicarious liability.*

Assumption of the risk states that participants, especially those in sports, know that there are inherent risks associated with sport participation. You, as a participant, must assume and realize there are risks associated with sport participation; for example, a participant in a football game catches a football pass and lands the wrong way and injures himself. Can you claim someone else responsible (coaches or players) for that injury if there was not a defender in sight? NO! Hence, you have to assume the risk in this situation.

Contributory negligence is another defense one can use if charged with negligence. You can claim that a person contributed to their own injury or negligence. For example, many athletes engaged in "horseplay" fully know their actions are not prudent and they did not exercise due care. Throwing down a football after a touchdown and injuring oneself from the rebound is a definite case for contributory negligence.

Comparative negligence claims an injured pary is partially responsible for his or her own injury. In comparative negligence the court splits up the responsibility for injury between the accused and the accuser. For example, using the previous scenario, a coach encourages players to spike the football after a score. Though the coach did not encourage players to injure themselves, the act was encouraged. Hence, both parties are responsible.

A final case of negligence, *vicarious liability,* deserves special mention here. In cases of vicarious liability, a third party, often an employer, can be accused of negligence. For example, you as manager at XYZ Health Club, knowingly hire an inexperienced employee to run your exercise prescription program. If a member improperly prescribed for exercise died of a heart attack at the club, you as the employer could be held liable for the employee's actions and the subsequent death of a member. A word to the wise—you as sport manager, for reasons of vicarious liability, are one step away from a lawsuit!

Intentional Torts

As the term implies, intentional torts are those wrongs committed by individuals with "intent" to do harm. There are a number of intentional torts that are found with greater frequency in sport-related cases. These are assault, battery, false imprisonment, defamation, invasion of privacy, breach of contract, trespass, and fiduciary duty. The following section further elaborates on these types of intentional torts (Terry, 1915).

Assault: In assault cases, one intends to produce fear in another individual and intentionally tries to harm another person physically. Examples of assault in sports can be noted in ice hockey, when one player high-sticks another in an attempt to intimidate him.

Battery: Battery causes physical harm to another but the intent to produce fear to another individual is not present in battery cases. In the case study, Don Fearnone was physically injured by the referee, however, the referee was simply trying to prevent Don from harming others. Hence, Don sued for battery.

False Imprisonment: Typically found in cases of false arrest, we see this type of tort when a spectator is arrested falsely for inappropriate conduct during sporting events or is suspected of carrying illegal drugs.

Defamation: When incorrect or defamatory facts are claimed by one individual against another, defamation occurs. The media coverage of sports personalities often provokes cases in which athletes claim that their character was "defamed" or harmed in some way. To prove defamation, the individual must prove statements were made in a malicious manner.

Invasion of Privacy: Found in cases where public disclosure about a person's private life occurs, those who claim invasion of privacy must prove that it was done so in a malicious manner. For example, exposing information about an athlete's sexual life-style with "reckless disregard for the truth" is invasion of privacy.

Breach of Contract: Failure to live up to the terms or conditions of a valid contract is breach of contract. A player failing to show for a game when perfectly healthy or failing a drug test may result in breach of contract by the player.

Trespassing: Intentionally breaking and entering a facility without proper authorization is trespassing. Fishing and hunting enthusiasts have, on occasion, ignored "no trespassing" signs in search of the perfect catch.

Breach of Fiduciary Duty: A person's fiduciary duty or responsibility is to dutifully and ethically represent another individual. Sport agents, for example, owe their clients (athletes) fair representation dealing with all contractual matters.

Defenses Against Tort Accusations

How does one defend against a claim of intentional tort? If the accused party can claim that those who are bringing the charges actually gave consent "freely" and "knowingly," then the possibility exists for legal defense against a lawsuit. For example, if one can claim an athlete made statements freely and knowingly to a reporter about his or her personal life, the media can publish such information.

If found guilty of intentional or unintentional wrong, the court may award monetary awards to those injured; it might order an injunction or cease operation of the organization; or in criminal cases, imprisonment might occur. What is the easiest way to avoid these misfortunes from happening? Prevention! The following section explains risk management and insurance policies, which will help you to prevent legal "mishaps" (Prosser, Wade, Schwartz, 1976).

RISK MANAGEMENT

Risk management is a special type of crisis planning aimed at preventing legal crises from occurring. It should be incorporated in your sport organization's overall crisis planning strategies discussed in chapter 4. All risk management plans must inherently ask the question, "What could happen?" The following steps will help to alleviate potentially dangerous situations.

> **Step 1:** Stay up to date on current legal trends or legislative enactments that apply to your industry. Subscribe to journals that supply you with this type of information. Attend workshops or inservice training programs that keep you current on your rights and responsibilities.

Step 2: Hire and train individuals to assure quality performance by your employees. Insist on certification, when appropriate. To assist you in proper on-the-job training, show films or videos which can be documented in court if necessary.

Step 3: Always insist on proper supervision and training of members, spectators, athletes or any group whose safety is your number one responsibility. Certain activities (i.e., weight lifting, swimming) require constant supervision.

Step 4: Is your equipment safe? Checked periodically? Is it up to date? Used for the specific purpose it was manufactured for?

Step 5: Are your facilities safe? Checked periodically? Designed properly? Used for the specific function they were created for? Are they maintained and supervised properly?

Step 6: Are all policies and procedures in writing? Are they comprehendible? Do you require written waivers for participants? Are they sport specific in their wording? Signed by participant or guardian when appropriate?

Step 7: Is everyone and everything covered by insurance? Facilities? Participants? Employees? Is it comprehensive? Are part-time employees covered? Did you check with your professional association to determine the extent and type of coverage necessary?

Remember, the key to effective risk management is to be proactive! Claims that changes would be too costly or you simply didn't know about the problem or did not know the requirements of a certain law won't stand up in court! (Wong, 1988).

TRENDS IN SPORT LITIGATION

Individuals can and will sue for anything or anyone! Once protected by the aegis of governmental immunity or respect for those in authority, managers no longer enjoy this protection against lawsuits. A knowledge of the following sport litigation trends will assist you in the development of your risk management plan.

1. The average citizen is better informed—about their rights and what to expect from an organization providing a service to them! They are familiar with any legal recourse they might have to, or want to, pursue. Remember, you're dealing with an educated consumer!

2. The "deep pocket" theory is alive and well! People will sue any and all parties in an effort to collect monetary damages. In any one lawsuit they will sue an employee, manager, owner, equipment manufacturer or facility architect or developer. The "oneness" can rest on any or all of these parties!

3. There are increasing numbers of lawsuits that claim the participant was not properly informed. This could involve training techniques, activity risks, etc; hence, the importance of written policies, procedures, and waivers which participants sign to assure they've been properly informed.

4. There has been a significant rise in player versus player, player versus coach/manager, participant versus equipment manufacturer lawsuits. Quality control to assure that the best instruction, supervision, and equipment is available to customers is a must!

5. There has been an increase in protection of individual rights. Protection of minorities, women, handicapped, and gay and lesbian rights are guaranteed by the law. An awareness of rights of these groups will also help to prevent violation of rights from occurring.

SPECIAL LEGAL ISSUES: ANTITRUST AND LABOR LAWS

The final areas the sport managers must be concerned with are **antitrust** and labor laws. Let's first examine antitrust. Two pieces of federal antitrust legislation, Sherman Antitrust Act, 15 U.S.C., Sections 1–7 (1982) and the Clayton Antitrust Act, 15 U.S.C., Sections 12–27 (1982). Typically, the fifty states have enacted similar pieces of legislation to these two documents to respond to any legal issues at the state level (Allison, 1974).

The Sherman Antitrust Act, comprised of two parts, deals with issues pertaining to free trade involving legal contracts or agreements between parties or businesses. The idea is to prevent monopolies by one business over other competitive businesses. Also addressed are issues of price fixing or selling below-cost in an attempt to drive a competitor out of business.

The Clayton Act was designed to regulate individuals' or businesses' conduct before they actually committed a Sherman Antitrust Act violation. It regulates any agreements, for example, that might force someone to discontinue business with a competitor before entering into an agreement. It also scrutinizes corporate mergers that might create future business monopolies. Perhaps two of the most famous court cases in professional sports was the case of the *American Football League* v. *National Football League,*

323 F. 2nd 124 (4th Cir. 1963) which allowed for the continuation of the newly formed American Football League. Claiming that the National Football League could not monopolize professional football, the court ruled in favor of the American Football League.

Also, in the case of *Los Angeles Memorial Coliseum v. National Football League,* 726 F. 2nd 1381 (9th Cir. 1984), the National Football League was again tested. Its constitution bylaws specifically forbade relocation of a football franchise to another city without the unanimous vote of the league. The Oakland Raiders wanted to relocate to Los Angeles and challenged the National Football League's bylaws. The court found that the constitution violated federal antitrust law and allowed for the move to occur.

A final area, labor law, specifically deals with many player and team-related contractual issues. As early as 1875, issues in professional baseball were popping up with the announcement by four Boston Red Sox players that they were signing with another club for more money. That move left Boston without four of its outstanding players. What followed this action were years of turmoil over collective bargaining issues, threats of strikes, not only by professional baseball, but the NBA, NFL, and the NHL. The National Labor Act created a National Labor Relations Board to regulate labor issues in professional sports. Strikes and player grievances (salary and general disputes) are monitored by the board, which receives direction from the components of the National Labor Act. (See Weistart and Lowell, *The Law of Sports,* for a more detailed explanation of this legal area and any other topics addressed in our previous discussion.)

SUMMARY

1. The 1960s brought about a dramatic shift in awareness of individual rights and a subsequent increase in litigation.
2. There are three branches of government: judicial, executive, and legislative.
3. The Bill of Rights contains the first ten amendments to the Constitution of the United States. An additional 26 amendments were later added to the Constitution.

4. The first, fifth, tenth and fourteenth amendments are most frequently cited when an individual feels their rights have been violated in sport.
5. When individuals feel their rights are violated or they have had a legal "wrong" committed against them, these wrongs can be defined as intentional or unintentional in nature.
6. Unintentional torts are otherwise known as negligence.
7. Intentional torts can be classified as assault, battery, false imprisonment, defamation, invasion of privacy, breach of contract, trespassing, or breach of fiduciary duty.
8. Prevention is paramount in avoiding a lawsuit. Following a risk management plan will help to prevent lawsuits from occurring.
9. The numbers and types of lawsuits continue to mount. Staying abreast of sport litigation trends and legislation will assist in curbing this "sue syndrome."

REVIEW QUESTIONS

1. Which branch of government is the law-enforcing branch?
2. How does common law differ from written law?
3. Which constitutional amendment explains due process rights?
4. How does one differentiate between federal and state jurisdiction?
5. Where does the word *tort* come from?
6. What must be proven to be found guilty of a negligent act?
7. How can one defend against an accusation of negligence?
8. What does vicarious liability mean?
9. How does assault differ from battery as intentionally committed torts?
10. What is the most important question to ask when developing a risk management plan?

Computing in the Information Age

■ ■ ■ ■ ■ ■ ■

CASE STUDY
The Case of Multiplying Maladjustments

Sunset Years Health Club, established five years ago, was enjoying a surge of popularity in the Florida city of Leisureville. Marketing efforts targeting senior citizens and the large increase in retirees to the region had brought the club good fortune. Even the future membership forecasts were looking bright, with the baby-boomers doubling the number of retirees by the year 2010. Also, with increased scientific evidence indicating that fitness leads to longevity of life and the decrease in heart disease, the health club idea was not a difficult one to sell to the people of Leisureville. Profits were up until a certain "high tech monster" was introduced.

Club manager Robert Forchange, after attending a recent fitness tradeshow, was sold on the idea of introducing computerized training and fitness programs to the membership. After all, the accounting and membership services departments were already developing database membership listings and budgets, why not try to introduce the state-of-the-art computerized programs to membership? They could see graphical representation of workout performance, nutritional needs, regular fitness evaluation, and personal health assessment. Robert set about convincing the club owner, Don Verywealthy, that this would provide a competitive advantage over other senior citizen clubs in the area who utilized older or outdated fitness charting methods. Don came up with the money for such an investment easily and gave the project a "thumbs-up." Two months later, Robert introduced the new computing system at a club open house. The members appeared awestruck with the complexity of the new system and refused to comment during the party. They appeared to be more interested in socializing than anything else. Robert attributed this lack of interest in the new computing system to the social concerns that members had at the time.

The following day, Robert noticed membership attendance was down at the club, but chalked it up to "the Monday blues." The following weeks showed a continual downward spiral in members' attendance. What made matters worse, Robert was hearing rumors of several members wanting to quit and that membership morale had plummeted.

Finally, at the monthly membership advisory board meeting, Robert blurted out, "What's the matter with all of you? You act like you don't belong here anymore?" Ellen Goodfriend, an advisory board member, exclaimed, "We liked the way things were, we understood how our individual fitness programs worked, and we didn't have to deal with those 'high tech monsters.' None of us have ever had to use a computer and don't have the slightest interest in learning. You have destroyed our fun leisure time!" At that, all the members applauded and Robert was in shock. Each of the board members then got up and left, leaving him in despair.

DISCUSSION QUESTIONS

1. *Was it a good idea to introduce the new computing system to the members of Sunset Years?*
2. *What could Robert have done differently when introducing the new fitness system?*
3. *What are the benefits of computerized fitness programs?*

■ ■ ■ ■ ■ ■ ■

INTRODUCTION

Everyone will agree that we are functioning in an overcommunicated society. As future managers, you will have to establish membership records, sales forecasts, marketing research, and accounting/financial statements, keep scouting reports, operate electronic scoreboards, etc., etc. In Chapter 9, we emphasized the importance of communicating in a multidimensional organizational environment. The computer is the answer to your communication prayers. It will help you process, organize, synthesize, and manage the information sport managers handle on a day-to-day basis. The following sections will tell you how to use the computer to assist daily management functions, how to select computer hardware, determine which computer software is best for you, and specific industry computer needs and applications. Most of all, you'll discover how best to avoid the Robert Forchange dilemma.

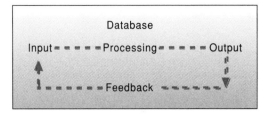

FIGURE 13.1
General operational
features of computing
systems.

SPORT MANAGEMENT COMPUTER SYSTEMS

How does one avoid computer phobia? How can the computer help you to manage more effectively? How did Robert Forchange err when implementing computer technology at his club? First, let's examine how all computing systems operate regardless of the application. Figure 13.1 outlines these ideas for you (Gannes, 1980).

When operating a computer, the process is always the same. Essentially, one must input information into a computer. Once inputted, the information computed is processed. The information computed is also referred to as a database. Finally, depending on what function you command the computer to perform, you receive a computing "output." For example, you may input a member's fitness performance levels. Ask the computer to calculate how these scores compare with average fitness levels of a person of their age and sex; the computer will provide you with an output that makes these comparisons. The feedback a member receives lets them determine if they are out of shape or operating at optimal performance levels. Imagine how much time this would take if you had to calculate all of this information by hand! The time you save and the instant feedback the member receives makes the computer a wonderful investment. Too bad Robert didn't explain the computer operation in a similar fashion to his members at Leisureville! He would have eliminated most of his headaches!

The computer uses that assist in carrying out day-to-day management functions in the sport environment is endless! Table 13.1 demonstrates just a few of the important management uses in both the internal and external organizational environments (Oeftering, 1987).

Table 13.1 depicts the many management applications the computer can assist with in day-to-day operations. A greater understanding of these

TABLE 13.1 Computer Management Uses in Sport Businesses

Internal Environment		External Environment
Business Operations		Customers / Clientele
Manufacturing Systems		Competitors
Accounting Systems		Government
Marketing Systems	Database	Suppliers
Personnel Systems		Technology
Management Information Systems		Economy

internal/external uses will assist you in your future computer purchasing decisions. The following sections elaborate more specifically on these special applications.

Business Operations

Sport managers that complain "I'm up to my ears in paperwork" certainly have not heard of the filing and retrieving, electronic mail, or word processing capabilities of the computer.

All organizational internal and external correspondence can be computerized, filed, stored and retrieved—eliminating tons of office storage space and organizational difficulties associated with paperwork (Dressang, 1987).

For example, word processing allows you to develop correspondence, modify it or make additions, without the use of paper. When the corrections are finished you simply need to print out the final draft, eliminating the frustrations from handwriting or typing documents.

Additionally, not only can you word process information but you can electronically send information through inter- and intra-organizational networking systems. Otherwise known as electronic mail, this computer application helps to bring any sport organization to fully automated operational levels. You can purchase in-house electronic systems to facilitate intra-organizational communications or fax machines which can electronically copy and send information to other cities, states, or even countries. Electronic mail transfers information from one computer to the next allowing different departments in one firm to communicate with each other. Fax (facsimile) machines operate very similar to a telephone attached to a copy machine. One simply dials the receiving party's fax number and inserts the page or pages to be transmitted in the copier. In a matter of seconds the receiving party has the document printing out of their fax machine. The timesaving advantages far outweigh the old conventional mailing and postal services which may take days or weeks to deliver valued information (Bulkeley, 1983).

Manufacturing Systems

An application more familiar to sporting goods manufacturers, computers have revolutionized the manufacturing sector, conserving on time, expense, and personnel. Computers assist in manufacturing design, production scheduling, cost accounting, equipment control, and inventory control. More specifically **CAD/CAM computing systems** (computer-aided design and computer-aided manufacturing) allow sport product designers to develop new product ideas. By simply using an electronic pen and television monitor, you can create product and material specifications. This system allows you to produce control tapes which outline equipment operations used in manufacturing the product just designed, all made possible through the amazing CAD/CAM system.

Accounting Systems

Knowledge of the "bottom line" is essential to successful operations in any sport organization. A critical application area, computerized accounting systems, help to account for sales and invoicing, inventory control, accounts payable/receivable, payroll, financial reporting, etc. Computer accounting information helps in budget preparation, tracking expenses and revenues, and the general financial "state" of a sport organization. It provides tangible, concrete information about the bottom line and why a firm might deviate from that line (Robinson, 1983).

Marketing Systems

Computers also assist in assuring the success of a firm's marketing efforts. If you recall from our discussion in chapter 11 on marketing, outlining the four Ps, price, promotion, place, and product, is a critical component of successful marketing strategies. Computerized marketing research assists in answering questions about the four Ps: What are competitors' prices? What are the best promotional ideas to attract target markets? How should we package our product or services? What are the best locations to distribute our products? All of these questions can be answered through marketing research efforts.

Computerized statistical analysis of data on trends and consumption rates in the marketplace not only assist with internal marketing management efforts but also the external management efforts outlined in table 13.1. Marketing research provides information on the economy, possible future markets, government regulations, competitors' characteristics and market position, and how to select new equipment suppliers or manufacturers (Dykeman, 1988).

Personnel Systems

Computers assist with personnel concerns by facilitating record keeping. Keeping records of training procedures, hiring policies and practices, employee policies, compensation programs, and employee evaluations help to assure organizational efficiency. Also by computerizing this information, confidential information can be kept confidential with coded files accessible by appropriate personnel only. Employee characteristics can also be accessed for government affirmative action regulations and future employee collective bargaining negotiations.

Management Information Systems

Management information systems (MIS) help to compile information needs to assist the basic management functions of planning, organizing, and controlling. Any pertinent information relative to these basic management functions are stored in MIS files and retrieved as needed.

The MIS file is organized in such a way as to facilitate decision makers at all management levels. Top-level managers, if strategically planning for a sport firm's five-year forecast, assess prior information on yearly plans, previous budget considerations, and organizational structure. Lower-level managers might require more operational information to facilitate operational decisions. This MIS organization is referred to as DSS (decision support systems) which simply classifies information in the file according to decision-maker needs.

HARDWARE: SELECTING THE BEST SYSTEM

The many computer applications certainly justify the purchase and use of computers in a sport firm's day-to-day operations. Which is the best system for your firm's needs? How do you avoid alienating your clientele as Robert Forchange did? The following sections describe hardware options available to sport managers.

Computer Hardware Systems

The most frequently used **computer hardware** system in the sport management field is a personal computer, commonly referred to as a PC. They are the slowest of the hardware systems because of the reduced size and processing capabilities. However, they are more frequently chosen by practicing professionals because they are the least expensive system ($500–$2,500) and easy to move and store. The most recent PC development, the laptop computer, is the size of a small briefcase, can be transported on airplanes fitting easily on a serving tray in the passenger seat. Popular PC and laptop manufacturers include IBM, Compaq, Apple, Hewlet Packard, Digital, and Tandy (Bralove, 1983).

Other available hardware systems include mainframe computers, which are more frequently used by large corporations. These computers typically service more than one user and are able to process large amounts of information at one time. However, because mainframes are costly ($40,000–$1 million) and require special storage areas, most sport firms do not have the usage need or finances for such systems. More popular manufacturers of mainframes include IBM, Digital Equipment Corporation, Control Data Corporation, and Burroughs.

Operating Hardware Systems

Regardless of whether you are using a mainframe computer, a PC, or a laptop computer, all essentially have the same components or parts and operate in similar fashion. Table 13.2 outlines this process for you.

As table 13.2 demonstrates, information is inputted through a keyboard, disk, or tape input device, visually displayed for the user on a monitor (known as a CRT, or cathode ray tube) and read into a **central processing unit (CPU)**. Input can also be controlled through a device called

TABLE 13.2 Hardware Operating Systems

Input Device	Central Processing Unit	Output Device
Keyboard	Control	Printers
Mouse———————→	Logic——————————————→	Plotters
Disks	Memory Storage Units	Video
Tapes		
Monitors		

a "mouse" which assists users with pull-down or window menu control options. A mouse fits nicely into the palm of a hand and is operated by rotating on the desktop until a cursor on the screen arrives at an appropriate menu command.

All CPUs have three basic units—*control, logic,* and *memory*. The *memory unit* is a primary storage area where all input information or data is processed and stored. The *logic unit* assists the memory unit by making data comparisons and calculations. More recently, RAM (random access memory) has replaced outdated CPU memory storage with the manufacturing of memory silicon chips. RAM memory units analyze information at a quicker rate with greater efficiency of operation. Finally, the *control unit* controls all the hardware operations (i.e., input commands, processing commands, and output commands). Control information is stored in ROM (read-only memory) which cannot be destroyed or changed by input data. ROM only dictates the control unit's operation and does not deal with the logic or memory units.

CRT display is limited only to the amount of information that will fit on a screen display. Therefore, printers allow one to view the finished document for correction or reviewing purposes. Printers come in a variety of shapes and sizes. They also provide the user with a variety of output opportunities. They can be classified as page (printing one page at a time), line (printing one line at a time), or character (printing one character, or digit, at a time). Another way to classify printers is by the way the print head strikes the paper. With an impact printer, the head *does* strike the paper; conversely, nonimpact printers have no paper contact. Printers will range in price from $100 to $1,400, so one must weigh the cost effectiveness when considering purchasing this output device.

Some popular impact printers include dot-matrix and letter-quality. The dot-matrix uses vertical wires or pins that strike against a ribbon, forming letters or characters. Letter-quality printers operate similar to a typewriter with a metal letter that hammers a ribbon to form a letter. Among nonimpact printers, ink-jet and laser are among the most popular choices. The ink-jet printer produces a jet spray of ink which dries immediately. The printer is slow but produces a variety of color inks for more colorful graphic representations. Laser printers operate on a tiny electronic laser beam which uses a toner to create near perfect letters or characters. The quality and speed of operation is superior to most printers, but so is the price!

COMPUTER SOFTWARE APPLICATIONS

Every individual who uses a computer does so for a variety of needs, a variety of reasons. To meet this great diversity of needs, an expansive number of **computer software** applications are available for purchase. It is important to note here that each computer purchased has a disk operating system (DOS) installed, which allows for only specific software compatible with DOS to work on that computer. For example, certain software programs will run only on the Apple computers, while other programs are only compatible with the IBMs. It is possible to purchase additional hardware to allow Apple software to run on an IBM machine, however, most people who purchase computers tend to go with a manufacturer that is most compatible with one's software needs (Elmer-Dewitt, 1988).

All available commercial software packages are categorized according to several broad need categories: general management, educational, industrial, personal, professional, scientific, specific industries, and systems software. From a sport manager's perspective, software categories more frequently purchased include database management systems (DBMS), word processors, spreadsheets, communications, graphics, and accounting systems. Let's examine further some of these specific sport management software applications.

DBMS software assists the sport manager with large filing and record-keeping needs. Used more frequently with mainframe computers that process large amounts of information and possess large memory storage capabilities, it has the power to maintain, organize, and update files. DBMS also allows for integration with other software programs which, for example, could perform a statistical analysis of this data for marketing research purposes.

Software manufacturers of DBMS include dBASE IV, R:BASE, or Clarion. Word processing software essentially allows one to enter, edit, and save text. Ideal for any type of correspondence—letters, memos, newsletters—word processors begin where the typewriter left off. Selected packages come with a spelling checker, thesaurus, grammar checker, graphic/desktop publishing options, in addition to the basic correspondence capabilities. Some of the more popular word processing packages include WordPerfect, WordStar, Microsoft Word, MacDraw, MacPaint, Aldus Page Maker, Ventura Publishers, Legend, or XYWrite.

Spreadsheet programs, otherwise referred to as worksheets, resemble a rectangular sheet of paper which is divided by vertical columns and horizontal rows. The row/column intersect is referred to as a cell. Spreadsheets allow for easy data entry using an accounting-type format. Most frequently used to solve cash flow problems, each cell or related cells can be given a "What if?" command. For example, what if sales decrease in quarter three and credit sales increase? A spreadsheet can perform the calculations for you! Some popular spreadsheet packages on the market today include VisiCalc and Lotus 1-2-3.

Communications application programs also assist today's sport manager. The electronic transference of data, downloading DBMS data for spreadsheet use, the retrieval of data from a library or another database all require specific software to operate. Additionally, certain hardware additions are needed for most communications systems to operate. Cables, phone lines, or modems are typical hardware to facilitate the operation of communication systems. A modem, modulator-demodulator, links a computer with a normal telephone jack. One can then dial the phone number of another computer and send information. Typical communications software applications that assist hardware use include: PROCOMM, Kermit, BITCOM, or PCTalk.

Graphics software adds another dimension to computer use and application. They go beyond the reams of paper with endless rows of numbers or letters. Pictorial representation of data, ideas, or concepts allow for greater learning enhancement and understanding. With graphic packages one can draw pictures or designs on a screen, design parts for sport manufacturing, and add color or even rotate a figure. Lotus 1-2-3, SuperCalc or WordPerfect have limited graphic capabilities. Harvard Graphics, Chart Master, Graph Plus are among the more frequently sought out graphic packages (Department of Commerce, 1988).

Finally, sport managers also benefit from accounting software usage. Software accounting or bookkeeping systems keep track of the bottom line in the organization through assistance with general ledger (financial statements) and other subsidiary systems such as accounts receivable/payable, sales, invoicing, inventory control, or payroll capabilities. A typical software package selected for accounting purposes is the Multiple Journal Accounting Software System.

Specific Sport Segment Software Packages

Whether you manage a health or corporate fitness facility, an arena operating company, or a sporting goods manufacturing company, you will use one or more of the previously mentioned software packages. Software selection, once again, depends on your organization's unique computing needs. However, there are some very specific sport application software packages available that deserve special mention here.

The club and fitness segment or industry has several packages available that provide a variety of applications. For example, packages may provide health risk appraisals, exercise prescriptions, class registration, locker management, guest tracking, facility use, nutritional planning, or exercise incentive programs. Some recommended software manufacturers include ClubWorks, CSI Software Inc., MicroFit, CheckFree Corp., or Club-Management Plus.

To assist in computerized arena and dome sport management, there are also a variety of application systems available. Packages assist in fulfilling the management needs of compiling sport statistics, ticket sales, electronic scoreboards, athlete registration, game-day analysis, or even analyzing athletic motor skill performance. Widely selected software packages on the market today include: SportsStats, Renaissance, Select Ticket Systems, MTD, and Data Flow.

Those in the sporting goods manufacturing systems primarily rely on software already introduced, CAD/CAM systems, which manage design and manufacturing demands. Other software systems allow for project management, investment portfolios, statistical analysis of market surveys, or sales forecasting. Packages known as Expert Systems provide information normally obtained from highly skilled specialists. Some selected software packages used to accomplish these tasks include: SalesEdge, Dow Jones News/Retrieval System, ThinkTank, and The Last One. Other systems with limited expert application capabilities include VisiCal, PFS Series, Symphony, and Framework.

To further assist your computing needs, there is a wide variety of computer journals and magazines which advertise and rate the latest in state-of-the-art computer software and hardware. Some of the more widely read periodicals include: *MPC World, Windows, PC Magazine, Byte, PC Computers, Mac World,* and *PC Windows.*

SUMMARY

1. Computers in the nineties help the sport manager to synthesize and organize the abundance of information they process on a day-to-day basis.
2. Some of the specific management computer uses include assisting with business operations, manufacturing, accounting, marketing, personnel, and management information systems.
3. The computer hardware system most frequently used by practitioners include personal computers, otherwise known as PCs. Other available hardware include mainframes and fax machines.
4. Typically purchased hardware input devices include keyboards, disks, tapes, monitors, and a mouse.
5. Hardware output devices include printers, plotters, or videos.
6. Computers come with a programmed disk operating system (DOS) which is compatible with software specifically designed to be run on DOS.
7. General software applications or functions include word processing, spreadsheets, graphics, and accounting programs.
8. There are also industry-specific software available to sport practitioners. Computer magazines such as *MPC World* or *PC Magazine* list the most recently manufactured hardware and software systems available.

REVIEW QUESTIONS

1. List the general operational features of computer systems.
2. What are some of the external computer application uses in commercial sport environments?
3. How can computers assist with overall business operations?
4. Explain how marketing research systems contribute to both internal and external marketing efforts.
5. What three basic units comprise a computer's central processing unit?
6. What is the most efficient printer available on the marketplace today?
7. Which operating system determines what software can be purchased for use?
8. List some specific industry software packages available for use in arena/dome management.
9. What are some of the more popular reference materials available to computer users?

Taking Special Issue with the Nineties

■ ■ ■ ■ ■ ■ ■

CASE STUDY
Hiring the Best (Wo)man for the Job?

Bum Cramer had been in this situation before and regretted making another tough decision. His all-male firm, Sport Marketing Consulting (SMC), was the top company in the city of Hotticket, Nevada. They specialized in developing marketing strategies for sport special events, such as boxing and wrestling expositions. Most of the top executives and managers handling these events were males and Bum attributed the firm's success to the loyalty of the clientele. Year after year, the same organizations renewed contracts with SMC until this past year, when Roger Shortsighted joined the firm as head of advertising. Roger quickly developed enemies with some of the major account reps. He was considered by many of the clientele to be too inflexible and conservative. As clientele relations eroded, Bum knew it was time for a change in personnel and fired Roger.

Bum set about to find a replacement and advertised in the city's two major newspapers. He narrowed the field of applicants to the top three candidates for the job. Barbara Radcliff was by far the most qualified applicant, with several years of industry advertising experience and an M.B.A. in marketing management. Bum was in turmoil. If he listened to his gut feeling, he could foresee more trouble with clientele and perhaps other male employees in the firm. However, logically, Barbara was clearly the most qualified and experienced applicant for the job. The two other top candidates were male, but presented clearly inferior credentials.

DISCUSSION QUESTIONS

1. *Should Bum hire Barbara and risk losing valuable accounts or perhaps cause friction with the employees of SMC?*
2. *What are the legal and ethical concerns Bum might have if he doesn't hire Barbara?*
3. *What are your suggestions for smoothing over conflicts if Barbara is hired as head of advertising for SMC?*

■ ■ ■ ■ ■ ■ ■

INTRODUCTION

The intent of this chapter is to introduce you to the major ethical issues and concerns that sport managers must address on a day-to-day basis. Women and minority acceptance as managers, marketing ethics, drug and alcohol abuse, violence in sport, and sports gambling are issues that constantly provide challenges for today's managers of sports. These issues will be addressed in the chapter and will allow for you to make more equitable and ethical decisions in the workplace.

WOMEN AS MANAGERS: A CASE OF NO SIGNIFICANT DIFFERENCE?

A study by Donnell and Hall (1980) that examined top executives nationwide found no significant difference in management effectiveness and performance between female and male managers. However, large differences were discovered in employee perceptions about males versus females as managers. Most employees viewed women managers as more aggressive, less likely to delegate responsibility, overly sensitive to criticism, and more abusive of power and authority. Why this negative perception when there is no significant difference in performance as managers? Additionally, why are there discrepancies in hiring practices and salaries reported in all private sector sport segments (Managed Recreation Research Report, 1988)?

Some plausible answers as to why women are perceived differently from male counterparts, hired less frequently, and paid lower salaries can be found in a recent study performed by Carpenter and Acosta in 1990. Both researchers conducted a twelve-year longitudinal study of 180 randomly selected colleges and universities nationwide. All were members of the National College Athletic Association (NCAA). The results of sport managers polled indicated that:

- 85% agreed discrimination exists.
- 79% agreed qualified women were not selected for positions.
- 70% agreed qualified women don't apply.
- 93% agreed "old boy" network was a negative factor in the workplace and in hiring practices.

- 91% saw poor advancement opportunities as a deterrent in applying for positions.
- 90% stated inadequate salary was a negative factor.
- 75% stated that stereotypes about women as managers exist.

Discrimination in the workplace prevails in spite of state (equal rights acts) and federal (equal pay act of 1963 and Title VII of 1964) laws which prohibit said discrimination. Sport managers openly admit that problems exist. Also, there are statistics to prove that it does, indeed, take place! So why does it continue? When a clear majority of managers are white males, lawmakers are white males, and law enforcers are white males, it is not difficult to see why the problem persists. You, as future sport managers, can work to change these negative trends by following some of these suggested management practices:

1. Strive to make the workplace a fair and equitable environment by providing equal job opportunities for everyone.
2. Focus on ability, skills, experience rather than gender.
3. Educate other managers about existing job inequities.
4. Provide inservice management training for all employees that will create opportunities for advancement.
5. Encourage more women to pursue sport management undergraduate and graduate degrees, which will make them more qualified for management positions.

The more that women enter into management positions, the more accustomed employees will become to working for a woman. Also, as women feel less pressure to prove themselves and concentrate more on job performance, increased success as managers will follow. Finally, with more women in management, there will be additional role models, encouraging other women to pursue such careers and providing less reason to discriminate!

MINORITIES IN MANAGEMENT

Another serious area of concern challenging sport management industries is providing equal management opportunities for **minorities.** Most minority job statistics that have been reported in the professional sport franchise industries have indicated large discrepancies between whites and blacks in management. With 54 percent of NFL players, 70 percent of NBA players, and 26 percent of major league baseball players holding minority status, one would expect an equal percentage of minorities in professional team management. However, this is not the case. When closely examining all categories of executive, head, and assistant coaches, and administration/ staff positions, only 6.5 percent positions in the NFL, 5.3 percent in the NBA, and 7.4 percent of major league baseball positions were held by minorities (Lapchick, 1986). Some cite the lack of degree completion by minorities as an obstacle to job advancement for minorities. Others claim that blatant discrimination prevents minorities from acquiring management positions. Whatever the etiology, steps must be made to deter further inequities in management of sports. With the efforts of Center for Sport and Society at Northeastern University that provides degree completion opportunities for athletes, more opportunities for advancement will ensue. Additionally, with the assistance of graduate and undergraduate programs in sport management that provide internship and job opportunities for these disadvantaged groups, they will soon gain the valuable experience necessary for advancement in these sport industries.

MARKETING ETHICS

Let's refer back to chapter 11 on marketing for one moment. As you recall, the purpose of sports marketing is to provide mututal gain for both the buyer and seller. Ultimately, most sport businesses achieve this ideal. However, there are exceptions to every rule and with these exceptions come deceptive marketing practices. The negative impact of these practices on society has forced tighter marketing regulations and an increased concern for marketing's impact on society.

Sports in particular is targeted with this problem because of the large sport advertising sponsorship by tobacco and alcohol manufacturers. The question many sport managers must face is, "Do I allow an alcohol or tobacco company to pay $50,000 to advertise at a sporting event when abuse of these products causes potentially harmful effects on an individual's health?" What is particularly troubling to sport managers is that the industry is in the business of promoting good health. Isn't allowing these companies to advertise contrary to these beliefs? Let's examine the following marketing issues, which attempt to answer these questions.

Social Criticisms of Marketing

The marketing ethics of the corporate world have long been under fire from society and not only for the conflict of interest issues mentioned above. Kotler, in 1983, lists several other areas of concern held by consumers in general. These include:

High Prices: The high price paid by companies to advertise products or services are passed on to the consumer by higher prices charged for the goods they purchase; for example, raising the price of memberships at a health club, passing the burden on to the consumer.

Deceptive Practices: Companies claim consumers are going to get something other than what the product has to offer; for example, claiming that purchasing a membership at XYZ Health Club will help you look like Jane Fonda or Arnold Schwarzenegger.

High-Pressure Selling: A common complaint found in the health club industry is high-pressure selling. Luring the unsuspecting clients into the door, the salesperson's only concern is closing the sale and not the needs of the consumers. Once the sale is made, consumers are left to fend for themselves, often without proper fitness and exercise guidance.

Marketing Shoddy or Unsafe Products: Ever wonder what happened to all the football helmet manufacturers? Why are there only two manufacturers still producing helmets? Many of those manufacturing companies who once sold helmets went out of business because of design flaws or the high cost of insurance.

Planned Obsolescence: Certain companies count on consumers growing tired of last year's clothing styles, thus maintaining a demand for new goods even though the consumer may not necessarily need new sneakers or a new sport attire. Some claim that planned obsolescence causes false wants and excessive materialism in consumers.

Cultural Pollution: The advertising assault on our senses is at times overwhelming. Everywhere we turn we see advertisements—TV, radio, billboards, newspapers, magazines, t-shirts, tennis shoes, headbands, etc., etc.

Excessive Political Power: When a tobacco company pays over $100,000 for a one-page cigarette ad in a sport or fitness magazine, what is the likelihood that magazine will publish articles linking cancer to cigarette smoking? The political power of corporate sponsorship should not be underestimated.

These criticisms have prompted action from the Better Business Bureau to tighten regulations and monitor industries more closely with respect to marketing practices. With this federal agency's close scrutiny in recent years, the sport industry has made improvements in areas of false advertising, discrimination of various consumer groups (handicapped, minorities), product safety, and high-pressure sales tactics.

Societal Marketing

Coincidental to improvements in marketing ethics, there has been the trend by corporations to refocus marketing strategies. Enlightened marketing, or **societal marketing,** focuses in on product value to the consumer and the long-run benefit to the consumer. Marketing from the consumer's viewpoint ("You are going to have to work hard to lose weight" or "friendly, courteous staff to assist your every need") has helped to reduce unethical marketing practices in our industry. Ultimately, the burden of decisions about marketing and ethical practices rests with sport managers who oversee such operations. Following societal marketing practices in your sport organization will not only bring in more customers but reduce customer complaints. Consumers will know you have their best interest at heart (no pun intended).

DRUG AND ALCOHOL ABUSE

The use of drugs and alcohol by participants, spectators, and any sport consumer has become a serious issue not only for sport managers but the entire sport industry. Substance abuse not only affects the personal health of your clientele but can become a serious liability issue for the sport manager. Serving intoxicated spectators that become harmful to others can shift the responsibility quickly to the manager who hired the employee who served the alcohol. A working knowledge of legal and illegal substances and prevention measures aimed at eradicating substance abuse will help to make your job controlling this serious societal problem much easier.

Effects of Drug Use

Table 14.1 lists some of the more commonly used drugs by society today. Also included are some of the ill-effects these drugs produce.

TABLE 14.1 Drug Use Effects

Type	Physiological Effects	Behavioral Effects
Alcohol (beer, wine, distilled spirits)	Impaired motor performance	Impaired judgement
Stimulants (caffeine, cold remedies, cocaine, crack)	Increased heart rate	Hyperactivity, anxiety
Narcotic Analgesics (morphine, heroin)	Increased pain threshold	Invincibility
Anabolic steroids (testosterone)	Increased lean muscle mass Increased blood pressure	Antisocial/Destructive behavior
Beta blockers (betacardone)	Reduced blood pressure Reduced heart rate	Depression
Diuretics (Lasix, Bumex)	Electrolyte/Fluid loss	Disorientation
Peptide hormones (human chorionic gonadotropin)	Increased muscle Increased bone mass	Increased masculinity
Marijuana (THC)	Memory impairment	Inability to concentrate
Hallucinogens (LSD)	Increased heart rate Increased blood pressure	Decreased attention span Mental confusion
Nicotine (cigarettes)	Heart/Respiratory disease	Addiction

Table 14.1 lists the most common drugs used by sport participants and spectators. Alcohol, more frequently abused by spectators because of its availability, has become a huge problem at sporting events. In attempting to regulate consumption at these events, the sale of low-alcohol beverages or discontinuation of sales before the final period of play has helped to curb the problem. The NCAA has taken a firm stance on this issue by prohibiting the sale of alcoholic beverages at all NCAA-sanctioned events. Early education programs and drug rehabilitation centers also help in the early prevention and control of alcohol abuse. Stricter criminal laws and fines for intoxication will also help to regulate this abuse in the future.

Cigarette smoking, banned in most public sport facilities, has helped to curb nicotine abuse by spectators. With recent findings of the harmful effects of cancer-causing agents and of inhaling second-hand smoke by non-smokers, great strides have been made in nicotine and tobacco regulation at sporting events.

TABLE 14.2 Amateur/Professional Sport Organizations' Testing Procedures

Sport Organization	Testing Policies	Banned Drugs
U.S. Olympic Committee (USOC)	Tests at Pan Am Olympic Trials	Stimulants, anabolic steroids, diuretics, beta blockers, sedatives, tranquilizers, depressants, alcohol
U.S. Powerlifting Federation (USPF)	Follows USOC testing guidelines	Stimulants, anabolic steroids
Major League Baseball (MLB)	Regularly and randomly tests MLB owners, managers, umpires, players with contracts containing drug testing clauses or individuals with prior drug abuse histories	Cocaine, marijuana, morphine, heroin
Men's International Professional Tennis Council (MIPTC)	Tests two random MIPTC-sanctioned tournaments; targets all players, staff, officials, and committee members	Cocaine, amphetamines, heroin
National Basketball Association (NBA)	Adheres to the collective bargaining agreement between the NBA and the NBA Players Association	Cocaine, heroin
National Football Association (NFL)	No regular testing; unannounced tests on individuals who are suspected of "reasonable cause" (believed to be using or distributing illegal drugs)	Anabolic steroids amphetamines
World Boxing Council (WBC)	Procedures similar to USOC	Similar to USOC list of banned substances

Drug Testing and Regulation Efforts

In an effort to regulate substance abuse by participants, most sport organizations have implemented drug testing and substance abuse programs. These programs have assisted in regulating the drug abuse problems of amateur and professional athletes. Table 14.2 outlines the professional organizations that have instituted such testing programs.

Testing policies along with drug awareness and education efforts helped in the fight against drugs. Employee inservice programs and consumer drug awareness campaigns are measures that all sport managers can take to create a drug-free environment in their sport club or organization (Newsome, 1989).

SPORT VIOLENCE

Yet another critical issue managers of sport constantly confront is that of **sport violence.** Many ask the question: Who is responsible for violence in sport? Players? Spectators? Officials? Managers? Owners? Sport governing bodies? The answer is that all of these inviduals play a contributing role in curbing violent outbreaks by players, coaches, and/or spectators at sport events. Your responsibilities as a sport manager assure all activities are conducted according to the rules and regulations of each sport. You hire the coach, who in turn selects the players and officials, who contribute to the "sportsperson-like" conduct required of all parties. Therefore, you are ultimately responsible (once again!) for ethical conduct of these individuals.

How do you define violence in sport? There are four categories, ranging in severity of conduct, listed as follows:

Body Contact: Physical body contact normally allowed by the rules of a given sport, i.e., checking in ice hockey, blocking in football

Borderline Violence: Penalized by the rules of a given sport, i.e., penalized for late hits in football, high stick checking in hockey

Quasi-Criminal Violence: Brings about serious injury, usually resulting in ejection from the game or suspension from play for a given period of time

Criminal Violence: A violent act so serious in nature that it could be classified as criminal violence, usually warranting involvement from the courts and legal system and resulting in lawsuits, subsequent fines, or imprisonment

Experts cite various reasons for the degree of violence exhibited in sports today. Some claim that society is responsible, that sports mirror society, that humans act out on aggressions, and that sports are simply another forum for this expression. An alternate explanation focuses on economic incentives. Spectators pay to see and come to expect violence in certain sports. The body checking in hockey adds to the excitement and spectacle of sports. Another theory poses the idea of the generic controversy, that there is an innate drive in all humans, referred to as "fight or flight" that causes us to commit hostile acts. Finally, the learning or behavior modification theory claims that players observe other role models or mentors commit acts of sport violence and modify their own behavior accordingly.

Whatever the etiology, the various sport governing bodies have tightened measures aimed at controlling sport violence. It is your responsibility, as a future sport manager to assure all responsible parties follow these guidelines which outlaw violent acts in sports. Assuring that everyone is clear on these issues (players, coaches, etc.) will help to make the playing field safer and easier for officials to monitor. This will provide for a healthy environment for players and a satisfying experience for spectators.

SPORTS GAMBLING

Executives from all the major sport governing bodies (NBA, NFL, NHL and the WBC) have combined their forces to strongly oppose the legalization of gambling in sports. One form of sport gambling, proposed by state legislatures, would be in the form of lottery ticket sales. State legislatures are interested in legalizing sport gambling from an economical standpoint—increased revenue for individual states. However, most do not buy this argument. To legalize something solely to increase revenue for a state seems ridiculous. Using that same logic, shouldn't states also legalize the sale of cocaine or prostitution simply to raise money? Sports gambling then becomes an ethical issue. The following concerns about the legalization of gambling will help you to formulate your own management position on this sports ethics issue. It would:

- increase attempts by players and coaches to influence the outcome of sports scores;
- create suspicion by fans who feel the outcome was influenced;
- change the nature of sport, focusing not on the beauty of competition but on the point spread;
- increase the number who are addicted to gambling;
- increase costs spent on monitoring and policing the league to preclude game fixing and point shaving;

- send the wrong message to the general public and encourage and promote gambling;
- increase personal health problems associated with gambling addiction (alcoholism, depression, suicide);
- increase crime (forgery, loan sharking, embezzlement, burglary, drug dealing).

The negatives of legalizing sport gambling far outweigh any monetary or consumer benefits that might result. A strong management position by those who coordinate any and all sport activities is required to ensure that the integrity of *sport* is preserved. You, as a future sport manager can add to the preservation of these ideals by incorporating a position against sport gambling into your management philosophy (Brubaker, 1990).

SUMMARY

1. Discrimination practices have limited womens' progress as managers in the sport management field.
2. Minorities have suffered similar obstacles that women have faced in the field of sport management. Future managers can impact these inequalities by demonstrating fair and equitable hiring practices.
3. Ethical marketing practices frequently questioned by professionals include the use of cigarette and alcohol manufacturers as corporate sponsors of sporting events.
4. Sport managers must constantly be aware of the impact on society of their marketing efforts. If we avoid high-pressure selling tactics, selling shoddy or unsafe products, or creating false wants in consumer groups, we can help curb questionable marketing practices.
5. Drug awareness and education programs targeting employees and sport clientele will help win the war against drugs.
6. Drug testing programs offered through the NFL, NBA, MLB, USOC, WBC, and the MIPTC will deter athletes from using illegal and harmful drugs to enhance sport performance.
7. There are several groups responsible for controlling violence in sport. Officials, sport governing bodies, coaches, players, and sport managers all contribute to maintaining a safe playing environment.
8. Legalizing sports gambling jeopardizes the integrity of sports.

REVIEW QUESTIONS

1. What percentage of women hold management positions in sports? Minorities?
2. List some of the obstacles to women and minorities holding management positions.
3. What are some social criticisms of marketing?
4. Name some of the more common banned substances recognized by professional sport governing bodies.
5. List some of the harmful effects of using anabolic steroids, cocaine, or heroin.
6. Who is responsible for violence in sports? List the varying degrees of both legal and illegal body contact in sports.
7. What is the major argument for the legalization of sports gambling by its proponents?
8. How would legalizing sport gambling affect the integrity of sports? What other negative social effects would result if gambling were legalized?

The Shape of the Industry

Application, application, and more application!
Part V culminates everything you have learned
thus far by making direct application to the
three sport management industry segments—
consumer, spectator, and participant. The
participation segment will cover participant
issues in health clubs, corporate fitness, and
hotel fitness facilities. Spectator concerns are
discussed in the section on arena and dome
management. Finally, consumer segment
addresses one of the fastest growing sporting
goods manufacturing areas, the athletic shoe
industry. This is about as real as it gets!

Choosing the Right Club
Multipurpose, Hotel, Resort, Corporate Fitness Facilities

■ ■ ■ ■ ■ ■ ■

CASE STUDY
"Launching a New Club"—Repositioning the Competition

DENVER CLUB DEFIED THE ODDS IN DEPRESSED MARKET[1]

By Carol Bialkowski

When executives from Amerimar Realty Management Company announced their plans to build a 62,000-square foot athletic club in the heart of downtown Denver, members of the local business community thought they were crazy. After all, it was the late 1980s and the Denver economy was depressed, the city was overbuilt, and there were already six clubs in the downtown area, three of which were over 60,000 square feet in size. Despite these contrary indicators, Amerimar forged ahead with its plans and launched the $8 million Athletic Club at Denver Place in April 1990.

The club opening marked the last major phase of development at Denver Place, a massive mixed-use complex which occupies two square city blocks in downtown Denver. The complex, owned and developed by Amerimar, also includes 1.3 million square feet of office space in three high-rise towers, a 1,600-space parking garage, a 335-unit Embassy Suites Hotel, 193 upscale apartments, a 95,000 square-foot enclosed retail mall, a day-care center, and a car-detailing facility.

The impetus for adding an athletic club to Denver Place was born in a tenant focus group, according to Tom Todd, general manager of the facility. "The owners got a group of tenants together for several days and asked what was the most important components they could add to the project. One was day care, which is a burning issue in Denver, and the other was a club." Despite the overwhelming evidence against the wisdom of building another fitness facility in the already saturated Denver market, Amerimar decided to give the tenants what they asked for. "The owners are very market driven," Todd said. "They give people what they want, kind of like how the Japanese build automobiles— what do you want and how much will you pay for it?"

In addition to the desires of the tenants, Amerimar considered several other factors before plunging into the construction process. A preliminary analysis of the competition revealed the six clubs in downtown Denver had gotten rather complacent and "soft around the middle" over the years. "They hadn't had a major competitor to challenge them in a long time, so they let the facilities get run down," Todd says. Translation? Their members seemed ripe for the picking. That the head of Amerimar is a fitness fanatic also helped the cause. "Otherwise, he just might have looked at the project from a cold, hard, statistical standpoint and decided against it," Todd points out.

Amerimar approached the launch of the athletic club with three major goals in mind—1) keeping existing tenants and attracting new ones; 2) increasing the average room rate and occupancy of the hotel; and 3) operating the facility as a standalone profit center. Early on, Todd realized that the company's tenant- and hotel-related goals had the potential to undermine the club's ability to turn a profit. "If someone is leasing 50,000 square feet of office space and wants free memberships for the principals of the firm, the leasing department is not going to say no," he points out.

To prevent the facility from becoming overrun with nonpaying members, Todd insisted that the leasing department pay the club for all "freebie" memberships given to tenants. "Otherwise I'd have 50 new members and no profit, and that's not the way to run a club," he says.

"I'm running this club as a for-profit center, not purely an amenity. And this place has a lot of overhead."

CRUSHING THE COMPETITION

Given that Denver's economy was in a slump and there were a half-dozen clubs in the immediate area, Todd knew he needed to "blow the competition away" in order to be successful. So he visited the other clubs, learned everything he could about their operations, and compiled a gigantic competitive research grid detailing the number of stair-climbing machines each club had, the size of their running tracks, the kind of strength-training equipment they used, and so forth. "I analyzed all of this information the same way Proctor & Gamble would look at Lever Brothers," he says. "Having come up through the sales and marketing ranks in big clubs, I look at it from a classic marketing standpoint—price, product, promotion, and positioning."

The result? Todd planned the entire 62,000-square-foot facility to counter the competition's weaknesses. Since the other clubs in town didn't have much open space or any windows in the workout areas, he designed the Athletic Club at Denver Place with high ceilings and surrounded it with windows. The competition's locker rooms were either on the small side or in need of a renovation, so Todd made sure the new club's locker rooms were plush, bright, oversized, outfitted with spacious grooming areas, and stocked with "every amenity known to mankind," including an iron, ironing board, and curling irons.

Since the other downtown clubs usually had waiting lists for cardiovascular equipment during peak hours, Todd went overboard in that area, purchasing one piece of cardiovascular equipment for every 25 members. "People who work downtown are in a hurry, and the last thing they want to do is stand in line for a bike or a stairclimber," he says. "If someone comes in to work out at lunch time, we don't want to frustrate them by making them wait. You can't afford to do that. We've never had a sign-up sheet for any piece of equipment. We just buy more." For the same reason, Todd spent $40,000 to $50,000 more than budgeted on machine weights, free weights, and circuit training equipment.

Todd discovered that none of the competitors had a swimming pool, so he put in a 25-meter indoor lap pool and an outdoor sunning pool.

The other clubs had small indoor running tracks; he installed a 10-lap-per-mile track. None of the fitness facilities in town offered fitness testing, so he purchased an elaborate computerized program. And the Athletic Club at Denver Place is the only club in the downtown area to offer free parking. "One club has parking, but you pay for it. That was a major competitive advantage," Todd notes.

Although the three big clubs in town have basketball courts, Denver Place is the only one with a basketball monitor. "When members go into the gym to play basketball they have to sign up with the monitor—first come, first served. One reason we do this is because one guy will sign up all of his friends before they even get there, and then they stay on the court for hours and no one else gets to play," he notes. "The basketball monitors are there during prime time to make sure there's fair play. If a member wants to form his own clique, he can always join the basketball league and sign up his buddies on his team."

Another major area of weakness among the competition was customer service. "By customer service I don't mean just a friendly person at the front desk saying the member's name. That's expected. We have people whose sole job is to walk around continuously, especially during prime time, and have a conversation with every single member," Todd says. "They're not taking people through workouts. They're just talking to members. We call it aggressive hospitality, and it's just not done in the other clubs." A pitcher of cold water and stack of cups help staffers break the ice with members. "As they're pouring the water they introduce themselves, ask how the member's workout is going and give them a chance to ask questions," Todd says.

MAKING MARKETING WORK

Before the launch of the facility last April, Todd staged a six-month marketing campaign designed to entice the general public to switch clubs. "We wanted it to be an easy decision," he says. But since the average initiation fee in downtown Denver was only $25, it was difficult to sell pre-opening memberships based solely on a reduced initiation fee. "If you offer a zero initiation fee they're only saving $25," he notes. So Todd hammered new members with a different premium each month, including logo T-shirts, logo sweatshirts, workout bags, even a pair of Nike cross trainers. Each month he raised the initiation fee $25 from a starting point of zero.

During the course of the six-month campaign, Todd sent out a total of 60,000 direct mail pieces. "One person came in with a direct mail piece in his hand and said, 'This is the fourth one I've gotten so I guess it's time to join.' That's what we wanted to hear. We needed to do this to get people to join," he notes.

The club also generated a sizable amount of publicity, as well as a fair share of memberships, through several major charity events sponsored prior to the grand opening. The most popular was a canned-food drive held in November which benefited the Denver Rescue Mission, a local homeless project. Todd offered new members $10 off their initiation fee for every can of food donated, up to a maximum of five cans. "It was a legitimate way to give people a price break. Some people would come in and bring 20 cans of food because they wanted to contribute," he recalls. "The Big Climb," a 31-story stair climbing competition to benefit the Leukemia Society, also was a hit with prospective members.

By the time the grand pre-opening party took place, the club had signed up more than 1,000 members. For the big event, Todd mailed 15,000 pop-up invitations to members and their guests, as well as a select list of community members. Nearly 4,000 people turned out for the bash, which featured a fifties band, a troupe of professional dancers, the Reebok aerobic dance team, and a DJ from the number one radio station in Denver. The bills for this extravaganza added up to more than $40,000, but since Todd generated $67,000 in memberships that night, the party paid for itself. "People still talk about it to this day. And that's the kind of thing that put us on the map," he says. The Athletic Club at Denver Place opened with 1,100 members and is expected to turn a profit this spring.

IRONING OUT THE WRINKLES

Although the facility's launch was successful, Amerimar needed to iron out a few potentially disastrous wrinkles along the way. A major obstacle was convincing its financial backers, including General Electric Pension Trust, the Robert M. Bass Group, and Balcor/American Express, to give the go-ahead for the project. "They didn't have to go out and get a bank loan, but it was still difficult to get the project financed because of the poor way clubs were faring in the country. It took two years of going to the partners, crunching numbers, and twisting arms to get the financing," Todd notes.

Once the club was in the works, a second major obstacle threatened to derail it. "The leasing people saw that we were selling so many memberships and they got nervous because they thought we would be giving away too many parking spaces to people who were paying $79 a month when parking was one of the primary incentives for tenants to lease office space," Todd recalls. When Todd saw that the leasing department was ready to pull the plug on the club's free parking, he estimated the number of members that would be using the parking garage in the morning, during the day and at night, and presented this information to the worried parties. "Then they backed off. I had cranked out 10,000 brochures saying we were offering members free parking for two and a half hours, and 5,000 of the brochures had already been sent out," he notes. "That was the single biggest threat we had. That would really have put a bad taste in the members' mouths."

Since Todd was the only person on the construction team who knew the ins and outs of the club business, a series of minor problems also surfaced throughout the construction process. "You had people building this who had never built a club before," he says. "Everybody hated me because I had a lot of change orders. I probably cost the project between $50,000 and $100,000 in change orders."

For starters, the locker rooms weren't designed with enough dry grooming space. "We had acres of lockers and nowhere for people to sit," Todd recalls. The plans for the aerobics studio called for a six-foot mirror on one wall, "and we have an L-shaped aerobics room. No one is going to do aerobics in front of a wall with no mirror, so I had them mirror every wall from floor to ceiling," he says. There also weren't enough electrical outlets for all the pieces of cardiovascular equipment Todd ordered, and there weren't any 220-volt outlets. "That was a big problem because I needed them for the treadmills, and a conversion after the fact would have been a big ordeal. So we put in a $12,000 panel just to run the treadmills," he says.

Problems cropped up during the construction of the basketball, squash, and racquetball courts as well. "They were going to put the wrong lines on the basketball floor. And the guy doing the squash courts didn't know the dimensions for an international squash court." Todd says. "They also were going to put the exhaust [vents] on the back wall of the racquetball courts, which is ridiculous because that's where the ball hits. So we ended up going through this elaborate process to put the exhaust in the ceiling near the back of the courts, but it was worth it."

"To them, these were little things. To me, these were big things," Todd continues. "The market was bad, and most clubs were losing money flat out. So I approached this club from one standpoint—it had to be the best it could be in every area. And I was a fanatic about that. If the lines on the squash courts were wrong, all the squash players in town would have thought we were jerks."[1]

■ ■ ■ ■ ■ ■ ■

The Athletic Club at Denver Place demonstrates a number of lessons in perseverance: six established clubs in the area, an economic recession, poor facility design coordination, luring away clientele from the competition, reluctance by investors to finance another failing club venture, adding to national statistics. Yet with all these hurdles, the Athletic Club persevered and became a profit-turning venture. How is profit achieved in this industry segment? The following section examines this issue.

---

[1]Reprinted by permission of *Club Industry* Magazine.

PROFIT=PARTICIPANTS

It is a well-known fact that to be a profit-generating operation in the club and fitness industry, the "bottom line" is membership sales. This concept presents itself in a variety of fitness settings. It might be the number of employees participating at a corporate fitness facility, the number of memberships sold at XYZ Health Club. Regardless of the criterion of reference, maximizing facility participation by present or future clientele is critical to successful club operations.

Equally critical to profit generation in this industry segment is clientele retention. A satisfied corporate client who continues to provide wellness programs for employees or members who renew yearly memberships at health clubs impact profit generation. Satisfied customers mean reduced advertising efforts. They spread positive comments about a facility, thereby referring new customers. They reduce the time and energy a manager must spend locating new customers or target markets.

The real question then becomes how do I provide the optimal facility to attract new members and/or retain present members? Let's explore some success stories in the fitness industry in this chapter. Voted by International Racquet Sports Association (IRSA) in 1991 as the top five club facilities, the following discussion of exemplary fitness facilities (Hildreth, 1991) will share some of their ideas on successful sport management strategies. Some have relied on suggestions found in previous chapters in this text. Others have used ingenuity and creativity applied to their given situation. Whatever the approach, you will have several operational foundations with which to launch your own success story in this industry segment!

EXEMPLARY FITNESS FACILITIES[2]

The clubs selected by International Racquet Sports Association as exemplary clubs in 1991 fared well in a number of categories: membership attrition rates, net membership growth, and operational profit margins. The clubs selected were from a wide variety of shapes (no pun intended) and sizes (12,000–55,000 square feet), had been operating from 4 to 16 years,

---

[2]Excerpts from Suzanne Hildreth, "The Superachievers: What it Takes to Become a Top Five Club" in *Club Business International.*

and were chosen from such facilities as a corporate fitness center, a tennis-only club, a multipurpose facility, and a family niche club. Collectively, what business strategies did all five clubs indicate made them a success in the industry?

- **Specific target marketing.** Focus on not being everything to everyone. Specific niche marketing worked best, offering specific niche services.
- **Tight controls on expenditures.** Revenues on the average grew much faster than expenditures, making these clubs much more profitable at a faster rate than average facilities.
- **Attrition controls.** These clubs exhibited an attrition rate of 27 percent while average clubs topped 35 percent, thus cutting down on advertising and marketing expenditures while maintaining a healthy cash flow.
- **Effective programming is critical.** The type, duration, and variety of programs offered at these facilities constantly keep members interested in the club and assures good participation levels.
- **Selecting quality, qualified employees is essential.** The top clubs claim employee excellence is key to successful facility operations.

Exemplary Club: Bel Air Athletic Club

Located in Bel Air, Maryland, this multi-purpose club emphasizes effective use of facility space. With this strategy in mind, they are able to achieve a gross profit of $75 per square foot. This is well above the industry average of $28 per square foot for multipurpose facilities. Built in 1980 originally as a racquetball facility, they responded in the mid-eighties to the changing needs of their clientele. They added a swimming pool, an indoor track, basketball courts, a sport-medicine facility, and a youth activity center. Their flexibility and creative use of space has allowed them to become a very profitable club.

Another major contributor to successful operations has been the employees. The Bel Air clearly tries to hire the right person for the job by using an extensive interviewing process that requires prospective managers to present a creative club project to all senior management. All employees receive a three-week employee orientation that covers club policies, procedures, philosophy, specific job responsibilities, and how their job coordinates with other employees in the club. They even have employees spend time with other departments so they understand each department's goals

and objectives. This experience also allows them to see hierarchical organizational relationships between departments and the mission of the
facility.

Exemplary Club: Frontenac Racquet Club

Located in St. Louis, Missouri, the Frontenac Racquet Club prides itself
on offering the very best in indoor tennis. Tennis-related offerings include
tournaments, lessons, social events, professional instruction, and apparel.
Their marketing targets two groups, young tennis prodigies who want to
develop their tennis skills and the over-50 market who desire a blend of
tennis and socializing with other members. The middle-aged market is
overlooked with good reason—they aren't interested in this type of club!

Facilities include eight indoor tennis courts, a pro shop, nursery, and
snack bar. They have seven tennis professionals on staff skilled at a variety
of teaching levels and able to meet the diverse skill needs of their clientele.
Programs a member can choose from include open court play by the hour,
league play, skill and drill clinics, couples and children tennis sessions.

The members must like something about this facility because they
constantly come back for more, giving the club a 9 percent membership
attrition rate! Their membership is yearly maintained at 1,000 to 1,200
members, giving them continued financial stability. Their overwhelming
customer goal is to be the "friendliest" club in town. It appears to be
working!

Exemplary Club: The Fitness Forum

Located in London, Ontario, this multi-purpose facility spans 35,000 square
feet and its middle name should be "programming." It enjoys an enthusiastic membership that can't seem to get enough of the facility or its
programs.

Offerings include 78 aerobics and fitness classes a week, ranging from
low-impact classes to super sweat and power jam aerobic classes. Special
program features include children's Christmas parties, fashion shows, dinner
dances, bake sales, recipe exchanges, ski and shopping trips.

They pride themselves in offering a relaxing, social environment, void
of junior members. With this marketing strategy and only permitting children in the club on special events, the facility provides members with "personal time" away from the kids.

Exemplary Club: Fitcorp Fitness Centers

Located in the Boston vicinity, this chain of nine corporate fitness and six public health clubs target the corporate marketplace. Some specialized service offerings Fitcorp provides include quarterly usage reports, on-site fitness lectures, corporation health profiles, and employee membership reimbursement by corporations. The reporting system developed by Fitcorp has helped to continually sell its facilities and programs to corporate clients.

Paramount to Fitcorp's success is its client orientation. Providing a clean facility and a friendly, servicing staff has helped these centers to become recession-proof and to achieve a successful reputation in the Boston area.

Exemplary Club: Club International Family Fitness Center

Located in Sante Fe, New Mexico, this facility has continually focused on what has made them successful—sticking to the fundamentals. This translates into providing a clean facility with the basic amenities: swimming pool, a wide variety of aerobic classes, strength and cardiovascular fitness equipment. Reasonably pricing their monthly membership fees from $28 to $34 also helps to keep their customers satisfied.

A centralized staffing system located at the front desk area also helps to keep all staff and management accessible. Service is paramount and has helped the club maintain membership growth. Success with these fundamentals combined with convenience and a relaxed atmosphere has also helped them to maintain a winning edge in the industry.

SUMMARY

1. In the health and fitness industry the key to providing a profitable venture is participation.
2. Fitness facilities understand profit is affected by retaining present members and/or attracting new members.
3. Underlying factors associated with profit through participation include knowing your markets, controlling expenses, low attrition rates, effective programming, and staff efficiency.

REVIEW QUESTIONS

1. How did the Athletic Club at Denver Place "crush the competition."
2. Compare and contrast IRSA's five exemplary clubs, outlining similarities and differences. Highlight what made each facility successful.

Life Under the Big Top
Arena and Dome Facility Management

■ ■ ■ ■ ■ ■ ■

CASE STUDY
"Is It the Place or the Show?
Dolphins Just Can't Win at the Turnstiles."

"IS IT THE PLACE OR THE SHOW? DOLPHINS JUST CAN'T WIN AT THE TURNSTILES"[1]

By Michael Mayo

MIAMI—Players are entitled to two complimentary tickets for home games, then they have to shell out like the rest.

So when Jim Jensen reached into his wallet last week for $360 to buy 12 more tickets for friends and family, he had a pretty good idea why there will be 52,000 people and 20,000 empty seats at Joe Robbie Stadium today for the home opener against the Rams (4 P.M.).

"You have to admit, for the average family it's very expensive to go to a game," Jensen said. "Parking, food, drinks, it all adds up. You can certainly understand that some people can't afford that."

Understandable, but still bewildering and disturbing. After all, the Dolphins are the state's most established and successful sport franchise. But their fan base has proved to be among the most fickle and apathetic in the league.

"I think it's very embarrassing," said Millie Petrillo of Plantation, secretary-treasurer of the Dolphin Booster Club. "I get more calls from other parts of the country and the world than locally. To me, there are more loyal Dolphins fans that live outside South Florida than in it. That's amazing."

South Florida's population has mushroomed since the Dolphins' glory days of the mid-1970s, but in five years at Joe Robbie Stadium, the team has drawn only two crowds bigger than 70,000. The lone playoff at JRS attracted 67,276; there were nearly 5,800 no-shows.

In 1970–1986, the Dolphins drew 45 crowds larger than 70,000 to the Orange Bowl. Dolphin officials are quick to use Hurricane Andrew as an excuse for today's poor crowd.

But season-ticket sales of 43,896, a 6.8 percent decrease from last year, are the lowest since the team moved to JRS in 1987.

---

[1]Reprinted with permission from *The Fort Lauderdale Sun-Sentinel.*

"Between the hurricane and the economy, it's just a tough time for South Florida," said fullback Tony Paige.

Of course, rising prices and flat teams have much to do with the lagging attendance. In most cities, fans turn into boo-birds when teams go sour. In South Florida, fans head for the early-birds, forsaking games entirely.

"We haven't been setting the league on fire, footballwise, the last five or six years," coach Don Shula said.

And yet the price of mediocrity keeps going up. The Dolphins raised most ticket prices for the third time in five years in January. Most seats sell for $30 and $28, although five upper-deck end-zone sections are available for $20 a seat. Those can be purchased for as little as $12 apiece through a promotion the team runs with Winn-Dixie Supermarkets.

But many fans and players think more price restructuring is needed. One suggestion: selling the top 10 rows for $15 apiece. As it stands, a top-row upper-deck seat at the 10-yard line costs the same $30 as a front-row seat at the 50.

Two other reasons for the lagging support: the transient nature of the population and the myriad leisure-time options available.

"Not to belittle the fans here, but they just don't compare to some other places," said Paige. "Look at the Redskins. There's like a 5,000-person waiting list for season tickets. I've been in South Florida for three years and haven't figured it out yet. I guess there's more to do: the beach, the water, fishing, golf."

"So many people are transplanted, so the Dolphins are only their second-favorite team," Petrillo said. "In most other places, fans support the team win, lose or draw. But here most everything depends on how the team is playing."

Although season-ticket sales jumped when the team moved to JRS, helped by club seats and luxury boxes, they have declined to the level of the last years in the Orange Bowl. The modern stadium and all its amenities are nice, but many players miss the charged atmosphere of the old stadium.

"We won an awful lot of games there; it's about as good a situation as you could have," said Shula. "Everybody was on top of the action and there was a feeling of tremendous fan support. Since we've been at JRS, there've only been five or six times that have come close to rivaling the crowd noise we had each and every week at the Orange Bowl."

Hot Ticket?

After the Dolphins moved to Joe Robbie Stadium in 1987, season ticket sales first jumped (from 50,729 in the final 8-8 year at the Orange Bowl), but have since declined:

Year	Rec.	Season tickets
1987	8–7	61,000
1988	6–10	52,000
1989	8–8	44,000
1990	12–4	45,570
1991	8–8	47,148
1992	—	43,896

Note: 1987–89 season ticket figures are approximate because exact count of club and luxury seats were not available.

■ ■ ■ ■ ■ ■ ■

PROFIT=SPECTATORS

The article in the case study points out how fickle fans can be and how the problem with fan "affiliation" runs deeper than we once thought. If you recall, from the IPM (involved profit model) concept first discussed in chapter 1, there is an inherent need for sport managers to recognize that the key to profit in the spectator segment is fan affiliation. The article attributes the lack of affiliation by Dolphin fans to several factors: ticket prices, the recession, Hurricane Andrew, the transient nature of the population

*South Florida's
major league facility,
Joe Robbie Stadium*

(the Dolphins are only their second-favorite team), the relocation of the franchise from the Orange Bowl site to Joe Robbie Stadium, and the deluge of leisure activities available to fans (water sports, resorts, travel, tourism.

How do you as a successful arena and dome sport manager improve fan affiliation at sporting events? Let's use three exemplar private facilities management companies and examine their facility management strategies: Joe Robbie Stadium, the Boston Garden, and Spectacor Management Group.

Exemplary Facility: Joe Robbie Stadium

Owned and operated by the Robbie Family, Joe Robbie Stadium is one of the premier arena facilities in the United States. Located in north Miami, the state-of-the-art facility plays host to a variety of events, from professional football and baseball to concerts, trade shows, and auctions. The 160-acre facility opened to the public in August of 1987 at a cost of $100,000,000 (Mon, 1992).

Designed by HOK Sports Facilities Group from Kansas City, Missouri, the stadium has a seating capacity of 75,000. The overall size of the facility is 648 feet by 736 feet and the playing surface is comprised of pre-scription athletic turf—designed to hold a firm playing surface even after

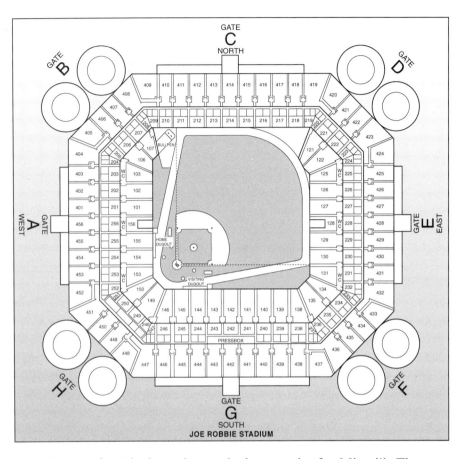

FIGURE 16.1
Field layout and seating
structure for baseball
at Joe Robbie Stadium.
Courtesy of Joe Robbie
Stadium.

30 minutes of a 1-inch-per-hour rain (a necessity for Miami!). There are forty concession stands (operated by FineHost Corporation out of Greenwich, Connecticut), forty male and forty female restrooms, first aid and security stations for patron and clientele use. There are 150 working press seats for football and 60 working press seats for baseball, with 10 radio/TV booths for football and nine for baseball. Lighting for the facility consists of 440 metal halide instant restrike light fixtures with 150+ footcandles at the playing field. The space usage for Florida Marlins baseball is 335 feet for the left field line, 410 feet for the center field line, and 345 feet for the right field line.

Figures 16.1 and 16.2 show the different field layouts and seating structures for baseball and football. As you can tell, the stadium was designed with multiple-usage events in mind—there is virtually no structure modification necessary to make the transition from football to baseball.

FIGURE 16.2

Field layout and seating structure for football at Joe Robbie Stadium.

Courtesy of Joe Robbie Stadium.

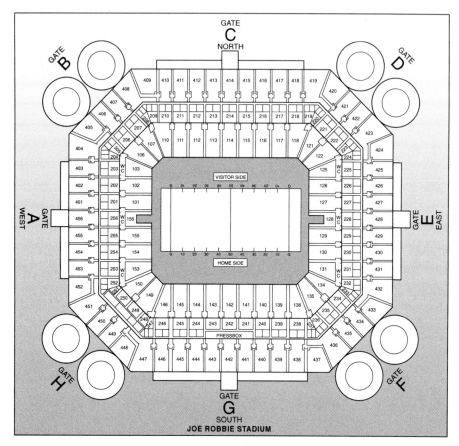

Exemplary Facility: Boston Garden, Delaware Corporation

The original Boston Garden was built in 1928. In keeping with Boston's provincial and puritanical ways, the facility was constructed with no air conditioning, no escalators, and plenty of obstructed spectator seating—almost as if the designers were saying, "We want you to suffer, life is suffering"!

However, the many magical sporting moments and ambiance of the Garden always seem to draw the sporting fan back for more pain. The multitude of championship pennants amassed by both the Bruins and Celtics only add to the unique charm of this facility—not to mention the sacred lucky leprechaun who lurks in the shadows!

Recently, the charm of the facility has faded to make way for the proposed new, upscale Boston Garden, just a few feet away from the existing site. Complaints about structural weaknesses, rats, and lack of fa-

A cross section of Boston Garden.

cility use during the summer months (remember, there is no air conditioning) has led to public outcry for a new facility.

The new Garden projects even greater economic impact on the community than the existing facility. Plans for bids on the NCAA Final Four, NCAA Hockey Finals, NHL All-Star Game, U.S. and World Figure Skating Championships, 1996 Olympic trials in boxing and gymnastics, and a national political convention in 1996 are just some of the projected income producers for the future Garden. Not to mention, if the leprechaun wants a club seat in the new facility, it will cost him $9,100 per year! Part of the "return on investment" equation must examine the cost-benefit of the existing Garden.

In tables 16.1 through 16.6, the overall economic impact of the current Garden is $66,707,682. This economic impact only covers 10 percent of the concessions revenues and no indirect revenues that the Garden might provide (increase in restaurant, hotel, small business profits resulting from events in the Garden). Given the cost of the new facility ($160 million, Becky Mattson, Development Coordinator, New Boston Garden, 1992) and benefit ($67 million), the new facility should be paid off in 2.38 years. The following tables point out specific economic impact variables that the Delaware Corporation must weigh in their decision supporting new facility construction.

Key Terms for Tables 16.1–16.6

Amount home team will spend locally— based on number of salaried personnel of the Boston Bruins and Boston Celtics who live in the metropolitan Boston area.

Amount spent— # (number) of people ✕ # (number) of days ✕ per diem.

Amount spent— total expenditures incurred by non-metropolitan fans (excluding parking) derived from # (number) of fans from out-of-metro area ✕ amount spent by non-metro fan = amount spent.

Amount spent by non-metro fan (exc. parking)— refers to what a fan traveling from outside of the metropolitan area will spend outside of the Boston Garden, excluding parking.

Amount spent per day by long-distance overnight fans— amount each person is expected to spend per day in Boston.

Average # (number) of tickets per event— the number of tickets expected to be sold per event based on knowledge of previous attendance records.

Average ticket price— ticket price per event based on average.

Category— the type of entertainment based upon spectator characteristics for the particular events. The categories chosen for the basis of this analysis were: family (f), general (g), scholastic (s), and sports (sp).

Concessions— the total amount spent by those attending games or events on concession items.

Concessions discounted— amount taken in by concessions that remains active in Boston's economy.

Daily amount spent by o-o-t media— amount each out-of-town media person is expected to spend per day in Boston.

Economic impact— the combination of direct revenues attributable to ongoing activities at the Boston Garden, adjusted to reflect the synergistic effect of reinvestment of revenues as well as increased employment in the area.

Grand total— the sum of all revenues having a direct impact on the local economy. For purposes of this analysis, gate receipts and a major

Key Terms for Tables 16.1–16.6
(*continued*)

portion of concession revenues were not included because these proceeds go directly to Delaware North, based in Buffalo, NY.

Long-distance amount spent— long-distance overnight fans per event × long-distance fan days × amount spent per day by long-distance overnight fans.

Long-distance fan days— the number of days × # (number) of long-distance fans X # (number) of events or games.

Long-distance overnight fans per event— number of people expected to attend games or events that will stay overnight in Boston.

Mass transit— the amount spent on public transportation by people attending games or events.

Multiplier— 1.88, which is 1.67 adjusted at an annual rate of 4%.

No. (number) of homes games— the number of games or performances scheduled to be held at the Boston Garden.

On-site advertising— amount spent on advertising seen from within the Boston Garden.

Parking— the amount people spend to park their cars at events or games.

Per diem— per day.

Team or event— the names of the specific programs taking place.

Ticket sales— the no. of home games × the average ticket price × average # (number) of tickets sold.

Total amount spent by o-o-t media— number of o-o-t media personnel × number of o-o-t media days × daily amount spent by o-o-t media.

Visiting team or event personnel spending data—# (number) of people: team or event personnel # (number) days: the number of nights expected to stay in Boston. Per diem: amount each person is expected to spend per day in Boston.

 # (number) of fans traveling from out-of-metro area— the number of people attending game or event from a distance outside of the metropolitan area that requires them to drive or take the commuter rail.

Key Terms for Tables 16.1–16.6
(*continued*)

(number) of local fans— fans living and traveling to game or event from within metropolitan area.

(number) of o-o-t media days— the number of days ✕ # (number) of out-of-town media personnel ✕ the number of games or events.

(number) of o-o-t media personnel— number of out-of-town media personnel expected to cover a particular game or event.

TABLE 16.1 Total Fan Participation for the Boston Garden

Category	Team or Event	No. Home Games	Average Ticket Price	Average # of Tickets per Event	Ticket Sales
f	Circus	21	15	8000	$2,520,000
f	Highlanders	1	20	2000	$40,000
f	Sesame on Ice	10	20	8000	$1,600,000
f	Wives' Carnival	1	10	1000	$10,000
f	Skating	2	20	8000	$320,000
f	Disney on Ice	12	20	8000	$1,920,000
f	Globetrotters	1	15	8000	$120,000
g	Wrestling	6	25	8000	$1,200,000
g	Concerts	6	26	20000	$3,120,000
s	Bean Pot	2	15	10000	$300,000
s	High School Hockey	5	10	5000	$250,000
s	High School Basketball	3	10	5000	$150,000
s	Hockeyfest	3	10	5000	$150,000
sp	Preseason Celtics	1	20	8000	$160,000
sp	Celtics	38	30	16000	$18,240,000
sp	Celtics Play-offs	15	50	16000	$12,000,000
sp	Preseason Bruins	0	15	8000	$0
sp	Bruins	41	30	15000	$18,450,000
sp	Bruins Play-offs	16	40	15000	$9,600,000
	Totals				$70,150,000

TABLE 16.2 Visiting Team or Event Personnel Spending Data

Team or Event	Amount Home Team Will Spend Locally	# People	# Days	Per Diem	Amount Spent
Circus	$0	200	12	$125	$300,000
Highlanders	$0	75	2	$125	$18,750
Sesame on Ice	$0	100	5	$125	$62,500
Wives' Carnival	$0	0	0	$125	$0
Skating	$0	75	4	$125	$37,500
Disney on Ice	$0	100	13	$125	$162,500
Globetrotters	$0	30	2	$125	$7,500
Wrestling	$0	50	12	$125	$75,000
Concerts	$0	50	12	$125	$75,000
Bean Pot	$0	0	0	$125	$0
High School Hockey	$0	0	0	$125	$0
High School Basketball	$0	0	0	$125	$0
Hockeyfest	$0	0	0	$125	$0
Preseason Celtics	$0	25	1	$125	$3,125
Celtics	$2,625,000	25	38	$125	$118,750
Celtics Play-offs	$0	30	30	$125	$112,500
Preseason Bruins	$0	35	0	$125	$0
Bruins	$2,550,000	35	41	$125	$179,375
Bruins Play-offs	$0	40	32	$125	$160,000
Totals	$5,175,000				$1,312,500

TABLE 16.3 Boston Garden: Metropolitan Economic Impact

Team or Event	# Local Fans	# Fans Traveling from Out-of-Metro Area	Amount Spent by Non-Metro Fan (Exclude Parking)	Amount Spent	Long-Distance Overnight Fans	Long-Distance Fan Days (Days × Fans × # Events)	Long-Distance Amount Spent Per Day	Long-Distance Amount Spent
Circus	6000	2000	$10	$20,000	0	0	$0	$0
Highlanders	500	1500	$10	$15,000	0	0	$0	$0
Sessame on Ice	2000	6000	$10	$60,000	0	0	$0	$0
Wives' Carnival	250	750	$10	$7,500	0	0	$0	$0
Skating	2000	6000	$10	$60,000	0	0	$0	$0
Disney on Ice	2000	6000	$10	$60,000	0	0	$0	$0
Globetrotters	2000	6000	$10	$60,000	0	0	$0	$0
Wrestling	2000	6000	$10	$60,000	0	0	$0	$0
Concerts	5000	15000	$10	$150,000	0	0	$0	$0
Bean Pot	2500	7500	$10	$75,000	0	0	$0	$0
High School Hockey	1250	3750	$10	$37,500	0	0	$0	$0
High School Basketball	1250	3750	$10	$37,500	0	0	$0	$0
Hockeyfest	1250	3750	$10	$37,500	0	0	$0	$0
Preseason Celtics	1625	4000	$10	$40,000	375	750	$125	$93,750
Celtics	3600	4000	$10	$40,000	400	30400	$125	$3,800,000
Celtics Play-offs	2400	9600	$10	$96,000	1600	48000	$125	$6,000,000
Preseason Bruins	1800	4000	$10	$40,000	200	0	$125	$0
Bruins	3375	7500	$10	$75,000	375	30750	$125	$3,843,750
Bruins Play-offs	2250	9000	$10	$90,000	1500	48000	$125	$6,000,000
Totals				$1,061,000				$19,737,500

TABLE 16.4 Boston Garden: Media Impact

Team or Event	# of O-O-T Media Personnel	# of O-O-T Media Days (Days × # Media × # Events)	Daily Amount Spent by O-O-T Media	Total Amount Spent by O-O-T Media
Circus	0	0	$0	$0
Highlanders		0	$0	$0
Sesame on Ice	0	0	$0	$0
Wives' Carnival	0	0	$0	$0
Skating	0	0	$0	$0
Disney on Ice	0	0	$0	$0
Globetrotters	0	0	$0	$0
Wrestling	0	0	$0	$0
Concerts	0	0	$0	$0
Bean Pot	0	0	$0	$0
High School Hockey	0	0	$0	$0
High School Basketball	0	0	$0	$0
Hockeyfest	0	0	$0	$0
Preseason Celtics	0	0	$0	$0
Celtics	0	0	$0	$0
Celtics Play-offs	100	3000	$125	$375,000
Preseason Bruins	0	0	$0	$0
Bruins	0	0	$0	$0
Bruins Play-offs	50	1600	$125	$200,000
Totals				$575,000

TABLE 16.5 Boston Garden: Yearly Revenue Generated

Team or Event	Parking	Mass Transit	Concessions	Concessions Discounted	On-Site Advertising
Circus	$21,000	$3,200	$840,000	$84,000	$63,000
Highlanders	$11,750	$1,600	$10,000	$1,000	$3,000
Sesame on Ice	$47,000	$6,400	$400,000	$40,000	$30,000
Wives' Carnival	$5,875	$800	$5,000	$500	$3,000
Skating	$47,000	$6,400	$80,000	$8,000	$6,000
Disney on Ice	$47,000	$6,400	$480,000	$48,000	$36,000
Globetrotters	$47,000	$6,400	$40,000	$4,000	$3,000
Wrestling	$47,000	$6,400	$240,000	$24,000	$18,000
Concerts	$117,500	$16,000	$600,000	$60,000	$18,000
Bean Pot	$58,750	$8,000	$100,000	$10,000	$5,000
High School Hockey	$29,375	$4,000	$125,000	$12,500	$12,500
High School Basketball	$29,375	$4,000	$75,000	$7,500	$7,500
Hockeyfest	$29,375	$4,000	$75,000	$7,500	$7,500
Preseason Celtics	$31,625	$4,325	$64,000	$6,400	$30,000
Celtics	$33,600	$4,720	$4,864,000	$486,400	$1,140,000
Celtics Play-offs	$74,400	$10,080	$1,920,000	$192,000	$600,000
Preseason Bruins	$31,800	$4,360	$0	$0	$0
Bruins	$59,625	$8,175	$4,920,000	$492,000	$2,050,000
Bruins Play-offs	$69,750	$9,450	$1,920,000	$192,000	$960,000
Totals	$838,800	$114,710		$1,675,800	$4,992,500

TABLE 16.6 Formula: Economic Impact

Grand Total	Multiplier	Economic Impact
$35,482,810	1.88	$66,707,682

Exemplary Facility: Spectacor Management Group

Spectacor Management Group (SMG) has greatly impacted U.S. and international arena and dome management during the last fifteen years. Founded in 1977, Spectacor has become the leader in arena and dome management in the United States. It has accomplished this feat by developing an impressive list of national and international clientele. Its business strategy is threefold: to increase revenues and event activities, reduce operating costs, and improve service quality (Sauers, 1992).

Its success has come from assuming management control of publicly-held facilities or failing privately-held arenas that have been operating at a loss and placing a drain on taxpayers and local community leaders. They draw from industry specialists in all areas of management and marketing facilities. These specialists are responsible for all aspects of facility management and yet accountable and responsible directly to the local community to whom they provide their services. They are also sensitive to community needs and interests and utilize staff and professionals from the community. This management "team" concept has been the key to Spectacor's success as an arena operating company. Spectacor provides its clients with a variety of services, including the following:

A MENU OF SMG SERVICES

PLANNING

Feasibility studies, market
  research
Five-year business plans
Operational input for
  architectural design
Financing and capital
  investment plans
Site selection
Financial analysis
Section of furniture, fixtures,
  and equipment
Staff selection and training

ADMINISTRATIVE

Facility programming
Financial projections
Management and operational
  system analyses
Development/Revision of
  operations manual
Evaluation of existing
  management
Selection of new management
Aid in transition for new
  management
Labor relations/Union
  negotiations
Analyses of subcontracts
Liaison with governmental
  officials

From Spectacor Management Group information package. Reprinted by permission of Spectacor Management Group, Philadelphia, PA.

OPERATIONS

Personnel selection and training
Client and patron services
Food and beverage operations
Merchandising, concessions
Security planning, event/non-event
Event management and staffing
Post-event critiques and follow-up
Day-to-day maintenance
Long-range preventive maintenance
Parking operations and staffing
Periodic operational reviews

MARKETING AND PUBLIC RELATIONS

Marketing research and planning
Event booking and scheduling
Event promotion and advertising
Event sponsorship development
Group sales programs
National and local media contacts
Community involvement programs
Advertising strategies, media buying
In-house advertising signage sales
TV-radio broadcasting opportunities
Employee relations program
Crisis public relations

FINANCE

Budget preparation and analysis
Accounting procedures, audit controls
Long-range capital improvement planning
Control of rental rates
Maximization of non-event revenues
Box office management
Ticketing distribution
Computerized ticketing
Development of profit centers
Insurance purchasing
Purchase procedures
Inventory controls

Spectacor also provides a consulting service to clientele involved in facility planning, architectural firms, and project managers. They work with these individuals using a four-phase process:

Phase 1: Programming—equipment needs, costs, location timetables;

Phase 2: Specification—specifications, document preparation;

Phase 3: Procurement—identifying qualified bidders and manufacturers;

Phase 4: Installation and coordination—selecting qualified bidders, verifying delivery, and installation of equipment. The menu of services SMG can provide a client is described on the following pages. SMG exemplary facilities are also listed.

The following pages highlight some of the exemplary SMG facilities.

LOS ANGELES SPORTS ARENA
Los Angeles, California

Seating Capacity:	17,000 seats
Exhibit Space:	Main Hall 110,000 sq. ft. 160,000 total sq. ft.
Parking:	6,000 spaces on site
Amenities:	Restaurant (300 capacity)
Ceiling Height:	65'
Floor Load Capacity:	2,000 lbs. psf
ADI Market Population:	12 million

The Los Angeles Sports Arena is host to some of the world's most noted and prestigious events.

Home of the LA Clippers of the National Basketball Association and University of Southern California basketball, it hosts many sports and entertainment events from Wrestlemania and Bruce Springsteen to the Ringling Bros. and Barnum & Bailey Circus.

The Sports Arena was the site of the 1960 Democratic Convention that saw the nomination of John F. Kennedy. It played host to the Cassius Clay-Archie Moore Heavyweight Title Bout in 1962, and more recently, was the site of the boxing competition for the 1984 Olympics.

From Spectacor Management Group information package. Reprinted by permission of Spectacor Management Group, Philadelphia, PA.

KNICKERBOCKER ARENA
Albany, New York

Opened on January 30, 1990, the Knickerbocker Arena is a multi-purpose facility hailed as the "crowning touch in the revitalization of downtown Albany."

The Knickerbocker Arena complex includes retail space, a 1,000-space parking garage and 51,000 square feet of exhibition space. A planned pedestrian skywalk will connect the complex to the Nelson A. Rockefeller Empire State Plaza, home of New York State Government. The Knickerbocker Arena's 17,500-seat capacity makes it the third largest multipurpose arena in the state of New York. It is the largest facility in the United States with an Olympic-size hockey rink.

From Spectacor Management Group information package. Reprinted by permission of Spectacor Management Group, Philadelphia, PA.

Prior to the opening of the arena, SMG assisted the architects and developers in determining the facility's operational configurations, prepared all bid specifications, and hired and trained all necessary personnel. SMG has booked a variety of events into the Knickerbocker Arena, including the Metro Atlantic Athletic Conference Men's Basketball Tournament, the 1992 NCAA Men's Ice Hockey Final Four Tournament, home basketball games for the Albany Patroons of the Continental Basketball Association, concerts, family show spectaculars, motor sports, and special events. Also, SMG has established a working relationship with Team USA, the USA Olympic Hockey Team, for games and international tournaments.

Seating Capacity:	17,500 seats
Exhibit Space:	51,000 total sq. ft.
Parking:	1,000 spaces on site 10,000 spaces within an eight-block radius
Luxury Suites:	25
Amenities:	NHL hockey rink Olympic hockey rink Portable basketball floor 20,000 sq. ft. of retail space Four locker rooms, seven dressing rooms, one officials' locker room Ticketmaster computerized ticketing system Two loading docks One drive-in bay (height clearance—13½')
Ceiling Height:	78' to bottom of roof truss 130' from floor to roof
Floor Load Capacity:	Unlimited
ADI Market Population:	1.3 million (14 counties)

ST. LOUIS ARENA
St. Louis, Missouri

Originally built in 1929 as the home of the National Dairy Show, the St. Louis Arena became the home of the National Hockey League's St. Louis Blues in 1967. Today, the Arena plays host to major concerts and family shows as well. The St. Louis Arena has hosted NCAA tournaments, Davis Cup Semifinals, and the 1988 NHL All-Star game.

SMG has improved the aesthetics of the Arena both inside and out with renovated penthouse boxes and a renovated exterior. In addition, SMG has improved community relations and instituted a new scoreboard and dasherboard advertising program which has generated more than $900,000 in additional revenue.

From Spectacor Management Group information package. Reprinted by permission of Spectacor Management Group, Philadelphia, PA.

Seating Capacity:	18,700 seats
Exhibit Space:	18,000 total sq. ft.
Parking:	3,300 spaces on site
Luxury Suites:	61
Amenities:	NHL hockey rink Portable basketball floor Flexible seating configuration Restaurant
Ceiling Height:	134′
Floor Load Capacity:	500 lbs. psf
Press Box Capacity:	50
ADI Market Population:	2.5 million

THREE RIVERS STADIUM
Pittsburgh, Pennsylvania

Three Rivers Stadium is home to the Pittsburgh Pirates of baseball's National League and the Pittsburgh Steelers of the National Football League. Located on the city's north shore, Three Rivers Stadium has broadened its appeal to include concerns by popular rock groups such as The Rolling Stones, The Who, Bruce Springsteen, Genesis, U2, and Pink Floyd. It has also hosted motocross races, tractor pulls, circuses, auto sales, and religious conventions.

SMG's operation of the stadium has provided more than $3 million in gross income from additional events. Under SMG, Three Rivers Stadium has earned a reputation as a financially competitive, professionally managed stadium. Fans and the general public alike now have a positive image of the stadium as clean, safe, and well maintained, with a courteous and professional staff.

From Spectacor Management Group information package. Reprinted by permission of Spectacor Management Group, Philadelphia, PA.

Seating Capacity:	60,000 seats
Parking:	5,000 spaces on site
Luxury Suites:	104
Amenities:	Restaurant (700 capacity) 3 meeting rooms (60–125 capacity) Closed-circuit TV Projection facilities 1 Diamond Vision video board AstroTurf 8 drain through field
Floor Load Capacity:	300 lbs. psf static load
Press Box Capacity:	Baseball Press Box—100 Football Press Box—300
ADI Market Population:	2.3 million

BROWARD COUNTY CONVENTION CENTER
Fort Lauderdale, Florida

Opened in the fall of 1991, the Broward County Convention Center is the focal point for conventions and trade shows in the greater Fort Lauderdale area.

The Convention Center is part of a complex that will eventually include a 2,500-car parking garage, an 850-room hotel, a 350,000-square foot retail shopping area and 250,000 square feet of office space. The Center also features three cruise ship terminals adjacent to the parking garage.

Prior to the opening of the Convention Center, SMG assisted the architects and developers in determining the facility's operational configurations, prepared all bid specifications, and hired and trained all necessary personnel. In addition, SMG was able to save Broward County significant money on the purchase of furniture, fixtures, and equipment for the facility.

From Spectacor Management Group information package. Reprinted by permission of Spectacor Management Group, Philadelphia, PA.

Exhibit Space:	Hall A—64,887 sq. ft. Hall B—43,018 sq. ft. Hall C—42,774 sq. ft. 150,679 total sq. ft.
Meeting Room Space:	Ballroom—20,020 sq. ft. 28 total meeting rooms—33,953 total sq. ft.
Ceiling Height:	Exhibit Halls—30 ft. Pre-function areas—16 ft. Meeting rooms 113 & 114—14 ft. All other meeting rooms—12 ft. Ballroom—25 ft.
Parking:	2,500 spaces adjacent
Floor Load Capacity:	Unlimited
ADI Market Population:	3.0 million

SMG International

Expanding their services internationally, SMG also provides similar services to an international clientele base. These services include management contracts, facility feasibility planning, and security, crowd, transportation, vending, and concessions management. Examples of their international management efforts follow:

SMG INTERNATIONAL

The extensive resources, experience, and manpower of SMG are now available worldwide through the London-based company, SMG International.

SMG International provides a rapidly expanding list of international clients with global expertise in consulting, development and management of stadiums and arenas, conference and convention centers, and trade and exhibition halls, tailoring each project to the unique demands of each market.

SMG INTERNATIONAL SERVICES
- Comprehensive management contracts
- Facility planning, feasibility, and staff training
- Worldwide sponsorship, marketing and booking contacts
- Security and crowd management
- Concessions, catering and novelty vending
- Parking and transportation management
- Event planning and promotion

SMG INTERNATIONAL MANAGEMENT AND CONSULTING CLIENTS
Londondome Arena and Exhibition Hall: SMGI is employed by the Royal Victoria Dock Development partnership to provide a market feasibility study and give operational design input to the development

---

From Spectacor Management Group information package. Reprinted by permission of Spectacor Management Group, Philadelphia, PA.

of the 20,000-seat arena and 25,000-square meter exhibit hall within London's Docklands. SMGI has been designated as the managers of the facility.

Sheffield Arena: SMGI was selected to be part of a professional team assisting the City of Sheffield, England in the planning, design and construction of a 12,000-seat arena and exhibition facility. Sheffield was the host city for the 1991 World Student Games. SMGI was designated as the facility manager.

Oslo Spektrum: SMGI is providing ongoing consulting services in a number of areas for the 9,500-seat multipurpose arena and conference center in Oslo, Norway.

Dusseldorf Arena: The City of Dusseldorf, working in conjunction with SMGI, is planning a 20,000-seat arena within the NOWEA Complex area. SMGI was chosen to perform a market research analysis, operational design planning, and to operate the facility upon completion.

ADDITIONAL SMG INTERNATIONAL PROJECTS:

Birmingham, England	Melborne, Australia
Dublin, Ireland	Sydney, Australia
Rome, Italy	Hong Kong
Gothenburg, Sweden	Kaosiung, Taiwan
Milan, Italy	Taipei, Taiwan
Auckland, New Zealand	

SHEFFIELD ARENA
Sheffield, England

The opening of the Sheffield Arena in the summer of 1991 marked the beginning of a new era, in Great Britain, of American-styled, multipurpose arenas designed to accommodate a wide variety of business functions, sports, and entertainment events. The unique design of the arena allows for maximum flexibility of configuration while providing a convenient, air-conditioned and safe environment with unobstructed sight lines for all events.

Particular consideration has been given to the needs of event organizers. In-house equipment such as staging, forklifts, video and graphics display units are all available. The permanent ice floor, box office and ticket distribution system, meeting rooms, dressing rooms, press, catering and office facilities are provided to enhance both the entertainment experience and operational efficiency, making the Sheffield Arena the most user-friendly facility in the U.K.

From Spectacor Management Group information package. Reprinted by permission of Spectacor Management Group, Philadelphia, PA.

Seating Capacity:	11,250 seats
Exhibit Space:	50,000 total sq. ft.
Parking:	1,500 spaces on site
Amenities:	Permanent ice rink Portable stage Portable basketball floor Four truck entrances Divisional motorized curtain Four team dressing rooms Four star dressing rooms Two press boxes Television interview room
Ceiling Height:	82.5 feet
Floor Load Capacity:	500 lbs. per sq. ft.—eastern area 300 lbs. per sq. ft.—central area

One final word—to successfully operate an arena/dome facility, the bottom line is spectators. Filling seats with satisfied customers has helped to create the success stories you just read about. If you recall our earlier discussion on fan affiliation, here is proof that the stronger or more positive a fan affiliates toward a team or event, the more seats are sold. Your challenge as a sport manager is to find out the etiology of their affiliation.

SUMMARY

1. Fan affiliation is the most challenging problem facing sport managers in facility management.
2. Joe Robbie Stadium is an exemplary facility because it is easily converted from football to baseball sporting events and has excellent design features including field drainage, lighting, media facilities, and ample parking facilities.

3. The Boston Garden was selected as exemplary because the developers were successfully able to blend the old with the new, offer events year-round, encorporate additional seating space, yet still maintain the Garden mystique.

4. Spectacor Management Group is the largest sport facility management consulting group in North America. It offers a variety of services from planning to consulting to facility operations.

REVIEW QUESTIONS

1. How does the involved profit model help to explain the "bottom line" in facility management?
2. What reasons were given for lack of fan support at Joe Robbie Stadium?
3. What were the sources of economic impact in the existing Boston Garden? How will these sources affect the construction of the new Boston Garden?
4. What are the indirect revenues gained from Garden events?
5. What is Spectacor's business strategy?
6. How has the management "team" concept been the key to successful facility operations at Spectacor?
7. What is the four-phase process Spectacor uses in its consulting services?

You Want How Much for Those Sneakers?

■ ■ ■ ■ ■ ■ ■

CASE STUDY
"The Athletic Shoe Industry—The Power of the Consumer"

No clearer a case of consumer purchase power can be found than in the athletic shoe industry. It is a prime example of "what's hot and what's not driven by consumer needs and wants." Is the demand for "hot sneakers" worth killing for? Reports of some teenagers actually killing for 150-dollar sneakers have prompted individuals to re-examine not only the price but the power individuals possess when they own a pair of Nike, Reebok, L.A. Gear, Converse, Adidas, or Keds (*New York Times,* September 30, 1990). What is all the fuss about? Let's look at past and current marketing trends in the athletic shoe business for some answers.

■ ■ ■ ■ ■ ■ ■

EARLY DEVELOPMENTS IN THE INDUSTRY

The major impetus behind the growth and expansion in the athletic shoe industry was the increase in sport participation in the 1970s and early 1980s. Companies began producing higher performance shoes and designing, manufacturing, and marketing a wide variety of competitive and recreational uses. They also became more diversified in their product lines offering athletic apparel and accessories which further complimented their shoe lines. Their marketing strategy targeted elite athletes who would wear and endorse their shoes. It was critical that their products also carry with them a strong brand name and high ratings in industry trade journals. This would assure an easier entry into a very competitive marketplace. The "pyramid of influence" marketing strategy is outlined in figure 17.1.

FIGURE 17.1
Marketing strategies
for the athletic shoe
industry.

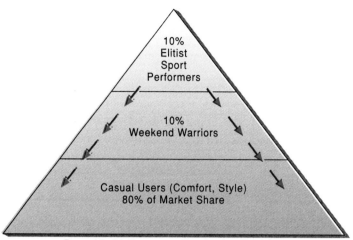

Pyramid of Influence on Purchasing Decisions

FIGURE 17.2
Athletic footwear sales.
Source: Data from Annual
Financial Reports.

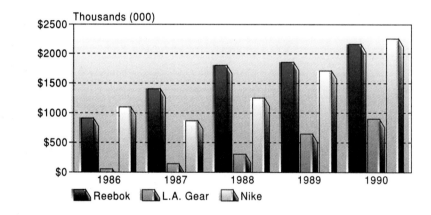

CURRENT INDUSTRY TRENDS

The 1990s saw a shift in industry leaders—from Adidas, New Balance, Etonic, Saucony, and Brooks—toward such companies as Nike, Reebok, and L.A. Gear. Nike edged out Reebok for the top spot in the industry with close to $2.2 billion dollars in sales in 1990. Reebok, close second, showed just over $2 billion in sales and L.A. Gear, a solid third in industry leadership with $900 million in sales. Figure 17.2 highlights the industry market share.

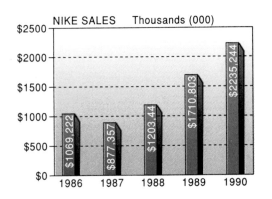

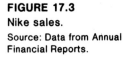

FIGURE 17.3
Nike sales.
Source: Data from Annual
Financial Reports.

What makes the top three tick? Nike, Reebok, and L.A. Gear have been chosen as exemplary sport manufacturing companies for the remaining discussion on sport product management.

NIKE

Nike began as a partnership in 1964 and incorporated four years later in 1968. They originally specialized in high performance running shoes. Today, Nike is the largest seller and manufacturer of athletic footwear in the world (McCoy, 1991), with revenues of over $2.2 billion in 1990 and revenues topping the $3 billion mark in 1991 (see Fig. 17.3). We will examine what has made Nike so successful, who their consumers are, and what the future may hold for Nike.

Nike Philosophy

According to Philip Knight, CEO, Nike's success is based on one simple philosophy: to produce the best possible products. To do this Nike has taken the lead in the athletic shoe industry and this has meant taking risks. However, these risks are not without rewards, evident by their three billion dollars in sales. Nike has always prided itself on producing a technically superior product. It is from this point that the discussion regarding Nike's marketing of products to the consumer must begin.

Target Markets

Nike is in a unique situation because they do not have a single target market, but rather many which they need to address in an individual manner in order to maximize sales. Nike offers an entire line of athletic footwear, ranging from basketball, golf, tennis, hiking, and running, to wind surfing, just to name a few. Within each of these lines Nike must segment a market, and in some cases, several markets within each line. For example, Nike makes running shoes for runners of all ages, but certain shoes may have specific appeal to the older runner because of added support while the high school runner's main concern is having shoes that are lightweight. In addition, Nike has also begun to add clothing lines to their product mix in order to attract new customers.

Youth

The first target market that will be discussed is youth. This group is comprised of individuals from infancy to 18 years old. In recent years Nike has taken a great deal of criticism for marketing their shoes to kids who can least afford them. Many people feel that by using people such as Michael Jordan and Charles Barkley, who are idolized by many black youth, Nike is creating a situation that is irresponsible. Most people agree it's the youth market that drives the fashion element in the athletic shoe market. While Nike does receive millions of dollars in sales from this market, they deny that they specifically market to this group. While Nike does not specifically market to children, it seems that their advertising has had a direct impact on this segment of the population.

Women

Currently, women account for roughly 42 percent of all athletic shoe purchases (Hayes, 1991). Nike has recognized this fact and has tried to devise a market plan that will best reach this growing segment. While women of all ages purchase athletic shoes, we are most concerned with the women between the ages of 25 to 45. As women in this age group have become increasingly active in a wide variety of sports, so too have Nike's marketing efforts increased. By marketing a cross-training shoe, Nike has been able to reach these women through one product rather than several. Once they have tried Nike, Nike is confident they will continue to purchase Nike products.

According to Lisa DeNeff, a spokesperson for Nike, "Women do look up to other women but they do not really have specific role models as much as men do." This led to an ad campaign that featured women in a variety of roles, from mothers to doctors, trying to achieve various athletic goals—with a tag at the bottom of each ad stating," "Just Do It." Nike has hoped that this no-frills approach will appeal to women in the 25–45 age group. With most women in this age group concerned with how they look, it is a good bet that this segment will continue to grow. By tapping this growing market, Nike hopes to remain atop the athletic shoe market.

In addition to this "new" market Nike remained solid in the male (age 25–45) market. Nike began using Michael Jordan as a spokesman in 1987, and since that time Nike has realized its greatest growth. While Jordan has contributed to this success, he has by no means done it alone. During this time we have seen an increase in participation levels of both males and females in the 25–45 age group. It seems that both men and women have recognized the high quality of Nike's products and are willing to pay for them. Couple this high-quality product and some clever marketing using major talent, i.e., Michael Jordan, and it becomes clear why Nike has been so successful. While a somewhat sluggish economy here in the United States has slowed the athletic shoe industry as a whole, Nike's overall outlook seems solid.

Financial Condition

During the mid 1980s the athletic shoe industry was going through some dramatic changes. This included a shift away from performance shoes towards shoes that were fashion orientated. In addition, the market itself was beginning to expand. We began to see people owning several pairs of athletic shoes instead of the traditional one. Nike had dominated the athletic shoe market for some time but now was faced with the fact that Reebok had overtaken the top spot in the athletic shoe market. In 1987 Nike signed Michael Jordan to endorse their new line of sneakers, and so began Nike's climb back to the top. Nike also began to advertise heavily during this period. The results of this campaign were an increase in earnings per share from .93 in 1987 to 2.70 in 1988 (*SEC Data Base,* 1991). During this same period Nike became very active in recruiting celebrity endorsers. They used Bo Jackson for their cross-trainers and Andre Agassi for their tennis shoes as well as Charles Barkley and David Robinson for basketball. By giving each one of these athletes a persona of their own, Nike was able to increase sales in all of their product lines. In conjunction with this, Nike began a separate ad campaign designed with women in mind. By using this segmented approach, Nike was able to increase sales in all of their product lines. By taking a look at sales, net income, and earnings per share, one gains a perspective on just how effective Nike's new strategy proved to be, (*SEC Data Base,* 1991).

Date	Sales (000)	Net Income	EPS
1991	3,000,000	279,400	
1990	2,235,244	242,958	6.42
1989	1,710,803	167,047	4.45
1988	1,203,440	101,695	2.70
1987	887,357	35,211	0.93
1986	1,069,222	59,211	1.55

Sales in the United States are, however, sluggish and many industry analysts believe that the athletic shoe market may be tapped out in the U.S. This has led Nike to international markets, which account for roughly 25 percent of Nike's sales (McCoy, 1991). According to Knight, "The Europeans are just beginning to view sneakers as casual footwear and not just something to jog in. "With Nike already having a strong toehold in Europe, their future has never looked brighter. Although the U.S. footwear market may be sluggish, Nike is continuing to expand their clothing line in hopes of reaching those 25 to 45-year-olds who may not be world class athletes but want to dress like them. Overall, the next few years should be one of sustained growth for Nike. They have positioned themselves in the market as the leader in the athletic shoe market and with continued product innovation and clever marketing should remain there for many years to come.

REEBOK

Reebok International Limited was organized by Paul Fireman in 1985 when he acquired the British-based company for approximately 500,000 shares of common stock (Moody's, 1991). Since then, Reebok has exploded onto the scene (see fig. 17.4), using diversity and a growth of subsidiaries including AVIA, Rockport, and Boston Whaler, to keep atop of the footwear

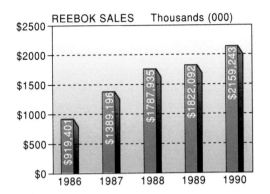

FIGURE 17.4
Reebok sales.
Source: Data from Annual
Financial Reports.

industry. Originally, it found early success as a fashion sneaker, but more recently it has boomed onto the athletic wear market with the advent of the "Pump." Since the invention of this marketing monster, Reebok has been on the cutting edge in the athletic shoe industry, dictating the styles and trends. Currently positioned as a strong second in market share, Reebok plans on gaining ground on industry leader Nike, based on the momentum of new technologies and products and the success of continued growth in a slowing economy.

Slowed growth in the marketplace and the recession has forced Reebok to focus more strongly on marketing and advertising campaigns. While the industry has steadily increased, it is a far cry from the double-digit profitability of past years (Bulkeley, 1991). The subsequent decline in growth has caused a dilemma in the industry—how to target new markets while maintaining balance in the old markets.

Baby-Boomers

Reebok has sought a solution to this problem by introducing new products to old markets. Specifically, it has, through its subsidiaries, targeted baby-boomers with an onslaught of new products, mostly along the casual wear line. A more aggressive ad campaign will be looking to exploit the 25- to 45-year-olds with such products as the "City Trails" casual footwear for women or the "F-16" casual wear for men. These new styles are meant to attract the athlete as well as the nonathelete, providing a filler for the gap that occurs in that time between work and play. While income limitations will hurt the industry's growth overall, Reebok is hoping to boost its sales through other such outlets for the baby-boomers.

In addition, the success of the "Blacktop" outdoor basketball shoe has attracted the attention of the younger generation, including teenage boys. This should help to further drain the disposable income of the baby-boomers as their children pester them into more purchases. By targeting the younger market as well, Reebok is seizing the opportunity to capture potential sales from the largest segment of the population, the baby-boomers.

Reebok also plans on continued growth in market share, due in large part to the expected decline of the smaller athletic shoe companies. Analysts speculate that, due to the dependence and subsequent expense of television advertising, only the "big two" (Reebok and Nike) will be able to afford to keep up the current pace. And while firms like L.A. Gear and Converse lose ground in name and product recognition, Reebok will gain in market share and sales (Pereira, 1991). They have besieged the market with "Blacktop" ad campaigns, an MTV venue, and Rockport marathon runners. These current trends can be expected to continue as Reebok battles for the top spot in the athletic shoe industry.

Reebok's Current Situation

In 1991, Reebok gained momentum according to second quarter published reports—earnings increased 39 percent on a 31 percent rise in sales (Bulkeley, 1991). This was a reflection of their strength both in the *international* market, where they doubled sales to $206.8 million, and within their smaller divisions, with subsidiaries such as Rockport showing dramatic gains. Reebok showed a 10 percent increase in footwear sales in the United States over the quarter, a figure that bodes more impressive in the face of the overall decline within the industry for the same period (*Wall Street Journal,* 1991).

While this data suggests improvement in the market, it is mostly a state of stabilization for Reebok on the domestic end. Until new monies can be found or new markets targeted effectively, Reebok can expect slow to minimum growth in the United States. However, internationally it is a different story. Based on their 100 percent gain in sales, the international market can be said to be a very promising venue for Reebok (Bulkeley, 1991). While Adidas still dominates the European Market with 50 percent of the share, Reebok can expect to see vast improvement in its marketing strategy and money management policies overseas in the next few years.

Five-Year Projection

As stated, Reebok can expect continued growth on the international market. Industry experts rate Europeans as they did Americans a few years ago, opening up vast potential in a virtually untapped market. As their market share increases overseas, their strength at home will continue to hold. One reason for this is their current financial position. Flexing its corporate brawn, Reebok has shown an increased desire to be in the picture for the long run by buying back 20 percent of its outstanding stock from the previous year. This is a major reason the EPS remained strong over the last couple of lean years, as shown in the chart. Currently, they have approximately 91 million shares outstanding, but that number can be expected to dwindle in coming years as Reebok looks to gain in financial stature (*SEC Data Base,* 1991).

Date	Sales	Net Income	EPS
1990	2,159,243	176,606	1.54
1989	1,822,092	174,998	1.53
1988	1,785,935	137,002	1.20
1987	1,389,196	165,200	1.49
1986	919,401	132,134	1.27
Growth Rate	23.7	7.5	4.9

The next five years appear promising for Reebok. They can plan on future success as long as the following conditions exist. First, the smaller marketers must continue to grow weaker during the recession, losing valuable ground in the fight for market share. Secondly, Reebok must maintain or improve upon their current financial stature. Third, they must continue to tap into the overseas market. Finally, they must stay on the cutting edge of technology, continuing to create new innovations and helping spur their growth during these lean years.

L.A. GEAR

Originally formed in 1979 as United Skates of America, Inc., L.A. Gear has taken advantage of every major trend that has swept across America, and California in particular. From the roller skating heyday of the 1970s, L.A. Gear has developed and marketed itself into the number three spot

FIGURE 17.5

L.A. Gear sales.

Source: Data from Annual
Financial Reports.

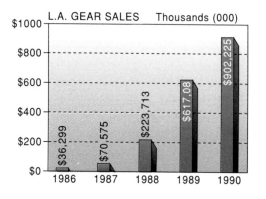

in the lucrative and highly competitive athletic shoe industry. L.A. Gear's official statement of purpose is designing, developing, and marketing high-quality athletic and athletic-style and casual footwear, as well as sports and casual apparel products and accessories.

In the mid-1980s L.A. Gear chairperson, Robert Y. Greenberg, began the climb to the top of the athletic shoe industry without much attention being afforded directly to athletics. Nearly 80 percent of L.A. Gear customers never set foot on or even near an athletic field or court. The company sold "sex and sizzle" to fashion-conscious teens with stylish aerobic shoes and brightly colored high-tops. These were not shoes on the cutting edge of athletic shoe technology but rather on the cutting edge of fashion. Nonetheless, they did serve as the catalyst for the company's rapid ascent in the field (Kerwin, 1991).

Early endorsements from *Sports Illustrated* super model Kathy Ireland and singer Michael Jackson demonstrate L.A. Gear's focus on the more fashion-conscious buyer. Greenberg and company began the drive towards capturing the market on competitive, high-performance athletic shoes. To chart the growth in sales for L.A. Gear, see figure 17.5. The success is evident in the climb from its fifteenth place ranking in 1986 to its current position which controlled an impressive 15 percent of the market share in 1990 (Grim, 1990). The edging of "veteran player" Converse in late 1989 demonstrates that L.A. Gear is serious about its new focus. But does the mere desire to be competitive merit the attainment of such?

Changing Goals of L.A. Gear

The athletic shoe industry has changed dramatically even in the past few years. The "Reebok Pump" and Nike's ever-popular air support system has created a market where buyers are well educated and not easily wooed by bright, flashy, fashionable sneakers that lack on the performance end. Unfortunately for L.A. Gear, the latter is a relatively fair description of the company's current situation. Although the new Catapult performance shoe, endorsed by the NBA's Karl Malone, has kept L.A. Gear in the race, the fact is that the company can spend only a fraction of the monies Nike and Reebok spend on research and technological advances. The result is that L.A. Gear's shoes have not met some tests of performance. College teams have complained of the shoes simply coming apart or, worse, blowing out during games or practices. These problems are not unique to L.A. Gear or any other young company. However, most young companies do not control such a substantial market share and have the expectations which Greenberg self-imposed on the company. L.A. Gear must capitalize on what made Nike and Reebok the ruler to which they must measure up: performance. The result is that L.A. Gear has had to take a unique approach towards its marketing efforts in order to compete with the veteran "big boys" of the business.

Target Markets of L.A. Gear

The change in focus from the California Valley Girls in the mid-1980s to the recent performance-conscious consumers demonstrates a change in target markets. No longer concerned solely with fashion-conscious teens, L.A. Gear has expanded its advertisements to account for the vibrant health awareness movement. As usual, a primary focus must be the abundant baby-boomers. The use of Kareem Abdul-Jabbar demonstrates the companies attempt to appeal to this generation who witnessed Kareem's ascent to glory from Power Memorial to UCLA to the NBA (Kerwin, 1991).

Recently dubbed the official shoe of the Continental Basketball Association (the NBAs minor league), L.A. Gear has not only seriously broken into the professional ranks but also reached out to a sport-starved market in rural America (Grim, 1990). Most CBA teams are not located in booming metropolises but rather in places like Quad City, MI and Albany, NY where local stars are admired and emulated. L.A. Gear has attempted to capture a very solid and plentiful market in these regions.

In addition to the baby-boomers, the CBA, and rural America, L.A. Gear has vied with Nike and Reebok with "guerilla" tactics in the big market. For example, for the 1990 Superbowl Nike purchased 90 seconds of air time to L.A. Gears 30 seconds. However, L.A. Gear's spot was immediately preceding the first half two-minute warning which is a peak viewing-intensive period. L.A. Gear, when competing with Nike and Reebok, must focus on this type of strategy. L.A. Gear simply cannot afford to go "toe to toe" against the seasoned and well-established market cornerstones.

Market Situation of L.A. Gear

L.A. Gear's success has been impressive but is it sustainable? Greenberg is, as usual, optimistic but facts seem to tell a different story. Recently, L.A. Gear has witnessed a decline in profits and overall performance. Although the company saw sales skyrocket from just over $32 million in 1986 to over $900 million in a recent fiscal year, they have also seen a decrease, from 1989 to 1990 of almost $24 million in net income and a fall in earnings per share from $3.01 to $1.56. This may be due in large part to the stagnant economy. L.A. Gear is suffering from an extremely high surplus of inventory which explains how the over $300 million in increased sales from 1989 to 1990 still resulted in a decrease in net income (*SEC Data Base,* 1991). However, there is more to the direness of this financial situation than current economic trends. L.A. Gear's rocketing to the top of the industry, although impressive, may have been somewhat premature.

The company's sudden shift to the high-performance athletic shoe industry, although following the American zeitgeist, was so sudden that L.A. Gear was unable to develop a product that would compete with the high-tech/quality shoes from the other big names. L.A. Gear is still in the relatively early developmental stage, yet is attempting to compete with the "big boys." Greenberg is pushing too far too soon. A brief glance at the company's current financial situation demonstrates L.A. Gear's inability to equitably compete with Nike and Reebok.

This brings the second and more paramount problem to the forefront. L.A. Gear has developed and thrived on hype and publicity. Due to the company's youth and limited funds for research and development, establishing "performance legitimacy" has been a major obstacle for L.A. Gear. Hype has taken the place of a quality product. The development problems that L.A. Gear has experienced are all part of the "learning curve." Quality products take time to develop and market. L.A. Gear simply needs more time. As one marketing expert put it "L.A. Gear is . . . finding that in order to claim performance legitimacy you gotta have legitimate performance" (Grim, 1990). Unless L.A. Gear can develop higher quality products which will appeal to the educated health-conscious consumers, the future for L.A. Gear is bleak.

L.A. Gear Summary

If the company maintains its current trends, the five-year projection for L.A. Gear is a sharp decline in sales and the loss of its current impressive market situation. L.A. Gear must maintain its focus on the baby-boomers and the rest of health-conscious America, but more importantly it must rid itself completely of its image as a fashion brand and become a respected member of the athletic shoe industry. This will only be achieved with the development of high-quality products. A brief fall from its current position in the market would not be surprising followed by a surge to the top once again. This time it will be to stay if, and only if, a quality product is developed that will sell based on high-quality performance and not hype.

ATHLETIC SHOE MARKET SUMMARY

As the athletic shoe market in the United States reaches maturity, the industry will see increasing competition for old markets that should force some of the lesser shoemakers out of the industry or into substantially reduced roles. Shoemakers will likely intensify their marketing and advertising efforts to keep their hold on old markets and expand into new ones. New product development will be very important as shoe marketers try to target groups such as the baby-boomers.

The biggest change in the industry should come from the increased emphasis on international sales. The potential for increased sales outside the United States is tremendous and the U.S. shoemakers have already begun to tap this gigantic market. Nike's use of such international stars as pole vaulter Sergei Bubka is one example of the increased emphasis U.S.

shoemakers are putting on international marketing. According to Andrew Mooney, head of footwear marketing for Nike, international sales could eventually become as much as 75 percent of Nike's sales as compared to their current 25 percent (American Marketing Assoc., 1991). In conclusion, the next several years should be very interesting as competition intensifies in the maturing U.S. athletic shoe market and shoe companies try to take advantage of the largely untapped European market.

SUMMARY

1. The popularity of the athletic shoe industry is driven by the consumer pyramid of influence.
2. Expansion in the athletic shoe industry, which began in the early 1970s, was positively correlated with the increase in sport participation.
3. The top three athletic shoe industry leaders are Nike, Reebok, and L.A. Gear.
4. Nike, the leader, has the most diversified consumer market and their strategy is to introduce the best possible product line.
5. Reebok's success can be attributed to the popularity of the "pump" and aggressive advertising campaigns.
6. L.A. Gear's success story can be traced to the "sex and sizzle" strategy directed at the more fashion-conscious buyer.
7. The future focus for the athletic shoe industry will be in international markets and sales which have previously been untapped markets.

REVIEW QUESTIONS

1. What drives the athletic shoe consumer?
2. What target market influences the buying decisions of other consumers in the pyramid of influence?
3. What were the estimated revenues for Nike in 1991?
4. How has the decline in industry growth forced Reebok to alter its marketing strategy?
5. What type of consumer makes up 80 percent of L.A. Gear's target market?
6. What consumer group will future new product development be focused on?

Sport Management

How to Never Close the Book on It!

IN SUMMARY . . .

This book has provided you with a number of suggestions on how you can successfully manage in the year 2000. Let's review some of the key management points covered throughout the chapters:

- Management depends on the *situation*—hence, there is no one best way to manage. You must pick and choose your strategies wisely.
- Planning is proactive, time consuming, and driven by goal setting. Management-by-objectives (MBO) provides the framework for all plans and the strategic plan drives all planning development for the organization.
- Organizing for maximum performance is directly linked to a business's strategic plan. Authority and power must match an individual's position in the hierarchy.
- Controlling operations requires hiring the right person for the job and managing a firm's financial resources wisely. Controlling successfully assures that the planning function is executed successfully!
- Decision making assures that all management functions are carried out effectively. WARNING: Never use a group for a decision that you can make yourself!
- Motivated employees are happy employees. Gearing your motivational strategies to an individual's needs assures productive, satisfied workers and greater harmony in the workplace.
- Effective communication strategies help to prevent organizational conflict and coping with change.
- All managers should be leaders. Effective leaders must be constantly aware of whom they are leading, the situational factors, and determine their preferred individual leadership style.
- You must be constantly aware of developments in high tech, legal trends, marketing ethics, and the constant societal events impacting the day-to-day workplace.
- Finally, to further complicate your life as a manager, you must realize that all these tasks and functions are INTERRELATED! For example, you can't motivate employees if you are not an effective leader; you cannot plan special events if you can't reach effective decisions; you won't be an effective organizer unless you can comprehend the skills and competencies of your employees!

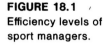

FIGURE 18.1
Efficiency levels of
sport managers.

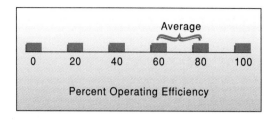

As you can see, the study of management is dynamic and lively! This book provides you with the tools to avoid management mediocrity and/or apathy. It provides you with ideals you should strive for in your individual management pursuits. However, reality seldom approaches the ideal situations created throughout this textbook. The following section explains the how and why!

YOUR SPORT MANAGEMENT REALITY CHECK✓✓✓

The typical sport manager falls somewhere between the 60 to 80 percent efficiency level (see figure 18.1). Managers below the 60 percent efficiency level seldom stay at one job for any period of time. However, what explains the inability for managers to achieve higher proficiency levels? Time management? Laziness? Incompetence? Lack of resources? Lack of formal training and education? Inexperience? All of the above? Let's have a "reality check" and see what prevents most sport managers from achieving higher proficiency levels in the many functions they perform. Management pitfalls to avoid follow:

- Management does not depend on the situation. Most managers operate from the premise that their way is the best way, everyone else must comply! It's simply too much work to assess the situation and employee needs.
- Planning simply satisfies self-serving behaviors and most managers are reactionary and don't respond to change well. Most goal setting comes from the top down, thereby undermining the whole premise behind management-by-objectives.
- Organizing and designing jobs are poorly executed and on many occasions altogether nonexistent. Departments and organizational design are often unplanned and simply a response to various work groups vying for power and control in the business.

- Controlling events and day-to-day operations are monitored by ease of measurability and visibility, or whatever makes top level management "look good"! Authority and power are often misplaced in the hands of individuals who are self-serving and egocentric!
- Decision making is spontaneous and reactionary. Many times work groups most affected by the decision are not consulted. Many managers consider this task to be the majority of what their job requires—i.e., trouble shooting and putting out the fires.
- Motivation in the workplace is still grounded in monetary and/or extrinsic rewards which are never individualized. Praise is often nonexistent in the workplace. Many managers never match goal-directed behavior with MBO (management-by-objectives).
- Communication in organizations are typically one-way, top to bottom. Very little consideration is given to the communication needs of the receiver and communication is not followed up by feedback.
- Selection of leaders is often based on traits, not behavioral or contingency methods. The primary objective of most leaders is to maintain the status quo, at the expense of progress or adapting to change. Productivity and emphasis on the bottom line supercedes consideration for the employee.
- Most sport managers do not have the proper computer training or skills to successfully run a business. Many do not want to attempt to learn these skills or to stay abreast with developments in the field.
- Managers are frequently one step away from a lawsuit and do not practice risk management. They simply respond to crises situations as they occur, increasing the possibility of legal entanglement and/or lawsuits.
- To many, marketing ethics is an evil word, using any marketing or sales technique that sells tickets, memberships, or products. The bottom line again is the primary business focus of most sport managers.
- The "good old boy" network is alive and well. This power structure promotes the practice of employment discrimination among minorities and women. White males still dominate as managers in the workplace.

- Drugs and violence are still as pervasive as they were ten years ago in sports. The constant finger pointing by managers, coaches, players, trainers, spectators, professional leagues, agents, commissioners, lawyers, sport-governing bodies and officials have left the sports world with no solution to these problems and no group accepting responsibility for their actions.
- Finally, most managers never clearly see how interactive and dynamic the functions they routinely perform are! In their pursuit of the bottom line they fail to see the importance of leading and motivating employees and how their happiness subsequently impacts the bottom line—how most employees want involvement in the decision-making process, how important this involvement is to management-by-objectives, or how proper planning can set the stage for successfully organizing, controlling, leading, communicating, motivating, and making decisions in the workplace.

How can managers who are guilty of management mediocrity avoid the pitfalls mentioned above? More importantly, how can you avoid inefficiency or mediocrity as a future manager? The following section provides some useful suggestions.

HOW TO BRING REALITY CLOSER TO THE MANAGEMENT "IDEAL"

Suggestion 1: Create clear, *realistic,* measurable objectives for management and employees. Establish a clear link between individual, management, and organizational objectives. ALWAYS, ALWAYS ALLOW FOR EMPLOYEE INPUT IN THE GOAL-DEVELOPMENT STAGE. Realistic goals are identifiable and converted into action more quickly.

Suggestion 2: Make all management accountable for not only their successes but failures. Managers are ultimately responsible for the successful operation of the business; placing the blame for failures on others is the first sign of management deterioration.

Suggestion 3: Individualize motivational techniques and reward systems. Never reward mediocrity or nonperformance! Encourage entrepreneurship and autonomy in employees. REMEMBER: Failure is never having tried!

Suggestion 4: Remember, you must always set a favorable role model. The old adage "Do as I say, not as I do" will not work! You are in a position to stimulate, motivate, and encourage employees. RE-MEMBER: Enthusiasm is contangious. Also, there is not an on/off switch for role models; this is a twenty-four-hour job, seven days a week. Consistency is key!

Suggestion 5: There is no room for a lazy manager! Success means going the extra mile, taking the extra effort to live up to high standards of quality as a manager. Management is not a nine-to-five job. Many times you are on the job until the work or task is completed. If you are entering the field for prestige or money, look elsewhere.

Suggestion 6: You will always be a *student* of management. Remember to keep an open mind about each situation and learn from each situation! If you make the same mistake twice, it's your fault, not a mistake! You are never too old or experienced to retool with the assistance of conferences, seeking advanced degrees or certification. This approach will provide you with fresh new ideas and a new way of looking at old problems.

Suggestion 7: You are in a position as manager to impact your effect or environment. This is your opportunity to make the world a better place by assuring safe, secure events for your members, clients, spectators. Improve the life-style and provide good entertainment value for your clientele. Create and adhere to ethical sport practices. Hire the best person for the job, not on the basis of color, race, sex, or religion but on ability.

Suggestion 8: Be willing to accept any challenge! Whether it affects your job or the workplace, make the most of every opportunity. Regardless of the obstacles or difficulty level, you must remember failing is not trying. Though there might be others around you who won't take up the challenge, remember Robert Frost's poem "The Road Not Taken." Take his message to heart and choose the path less traveled.

THIS IS YOUR CHANCE—GO OUT AND MAKE IT HAPPEN!

A P P E N D I X   A

Multi-Purpose Clubs

Income Statement	1991	1990	% Change	% Rev 1991
Initiation Fees	$ 107,619	$ 109,238	−1%	6%
Membership Dues	$1,291,492	$1,182,830	9%	68%
Guest Fees	$ 25,549	$ 24,805	3%	1%
Racquet Sports	$ 120,324	$ 113,483	6%	6%
Fitness & Dance	$ 33,699	$ 25,286	33%	2%
Service & Programs	$ 222,398	$ 199,122	12%	12%
Other Revenue	$ 89,266	$ 83,706	7%	5%
Total Revenue	$1,890,347	$1,738,470	9%	100%
Racquet Sports	$ 62,795	$ 56,349	11%	3%
Fitness & Dance	$ 109,295	$ 96,849	13%	6%
Service & Programs	$ 194,395	$ 180,938	7%	10%
Other Service Costs	$ 125,428	$ 114,085	10%	7%
Facility Operating Costs	$ 261,139	$ 240,099	9%	14%
Marketing / Sales Costs	$ 114,664	$ 117,109	−2%	6%
General Administrative Costs	$ 385,360	$ 363,613	6%	20%
Total Operating Expenses *	$1,253,076	$1,169,042	7%	66%
Net Operating Income	$ 637,271	$ 569,428	12%	34%
Fixed Expenses	$ 483,987	$ 473,264	2%	26%
Net Profit Before Taxes	$ 153,284	$ 96,164	59%	8%

Multi-Purpose Clubs (*continued*)

Balance Sheet	1991	1990	% Change	% Rev 1991
Cash & Equivalents	$ 62,484	$ 58,289	7%	
Accounts Receivable	$ 62,195	$ 57,157	9%	
Other Current Assets	$ 35,473	$ 28,198	26%	
Property & Equipment	$1,702,265	$1,709,735	−0.4%	
Less: Accumulated Depreciation	($ 591,639)	($ 529,880)	12%	
Total Other Assets	$ 111,142	$ 96,142	16%	
TOTAL ASSETS	**$1,381,920**	**$1,419,641**	−3%	
Accounts Payable	$ 47,471	$ 40,219	18%	
Deferred Revenue	$ 75,011	$ 76,251	−2%	
Other Current Liabilities	$ 132,967	$ 181,562	−27%	
Total Long-term Debt	$ 931,184	$ 888,202	5%	
Total Net Worth	$ 195,287	$ 233,407	−16%	
TOTAL LIABILITIES & WORTH	**$1,381,920**	**$1,419,641**	−3%	

*Operating expenses include payroll within each category. The total payroll for this group was 36% in 1991 and in 1990. © 1992 International Racket Sport Association, The Association of Quality Clubs, Boston, MA.

APPENDIX B

"Lost at Sea" Answer and Rationale Sheet'

According to the "experts," the basic supplies needed when a person is stranded in mid-ocean are articles to attract attention and articles to aid survival *until rescuers arrive*. Articles for navigation are of little importance. Even if a small life raft were capable of reaching land, it would be impossible to store enough food and water to subsist during that period of time. Therefore, of primary importance are the shaving mirror and the two-gallon can of oil-gas mixture. These items could be used for signaling air-sea rescue. Of secondary importance are items such as water and food, e.g., the case of Army C rations.

A brief rationale is provided for the ranking of each item. These brief explanations obviously do not represent all of the potential uses for the specified items but, rather, the primary importance of each.

1. **Shaving mirror**
   Critical for signaling air-sea rescue.
2. **Two-gallon can of oil-gas mixture**
   Critical for signaling—the oil-gas mixture will float on the water and could be ignited with a dollar bill and a match (obviously, outside the raft).
3. **Five-gallon can of water**
   Necessary to replenish loss by perspiring, etc.
4. **One case of U.S. Army C rations**
   Provides basic food intake.

"Lost at Sea" Answer and Rationale Sheet*
(continued)

5. Twenty square feet of opaque plastic
Utilized to collect rainwater, provide shelter from the elements.

6. Two boxes of chocolate bars
A reserve food supply.

7. Fishing kit
Ranked lower than the candy bars because "one bird in the hand is worth two in the bush." There is no assurance that you will catch any fish.

8. Fifteen feet of nylon rope
May be used to lash equipment together to prevent it from falling overboard.

9. Floating seat cushion
If someone fell overboard, it could function as a life preserver.

10. Shark repellent
Obvious.

11. One quart of 160-proof Puerto Rican rum
Contains 80 percent alcohol—enough to use as a potential antiseptic for any injuries incurred; of little value otherwise; will cause dehydration if ingested.

12. Small transistor radio
Of little value since there is no transmitter (unfortunately, you are out of range of your favorite AM radio stations).

13. Maps of the Pacific Ocean
Worthless without additional navigational equipment—it does not really matter where you are but where the rescuers are.

14. Mosquito netting
There are no mosquitoes in the mid-Pacific.

15. Sextant
Without tables and a chronometer, relatively useless.

The basic rationale for ranking signaling devices above life-sustaining items (food and water) is that without signaling devices there is almost no chance of being spotted and rescued. Furthermore, most rescues occur during the first thirty-six hours, and one can survive without food and water during this period.

---

*Officers of the United States Merchant Marines ranked the fifteen items and provided the "correct" solution to the task.

GLOSSARY

Advertising Paid forms of announcements, such as television commercials, billboards, or brochures.

Antitrust Laws preventing unlawful monopolies over trade by a business.

Authority Legitimate power stated in one's job description.

Behavioral Approach A management theory that focuses on the importance of understanding human behavior when managing employees.

CAD/CAM Computing Systems Computer-aided design and computer-aided manufacturing which assist sport businesses with cost accounting, equipment, and inventory control.

Central Processing Unit (CPU) Houses the control, logic, and memory units of the hardware operating system.

Classical Approach A management theory that believes a manager's work involves planning, organizing, and controlling.

Classical Design Theory Organizational structures that contain a formal chain of command, clear-cut division of labor, and centralized authority.

Clientele A specific group of consumers serviced by a business.

Computer Hardware Typically includes monitor, printer, and central processing unit.

Computer Software Computer application packages that fulfill a sport managers computing needs from word processing to graphics and accounting systems.

Concurrent Control Control functions that are executed on a day-to-day basis, i.e., monitoring employee performance, budget maintenance, monitoring supplies and equipment needs.

Contingency Approach Recognizing that management depends on situational factors such as: management style, employees, and the management decision involved.

Contingency Leadership Theory The leadership theory that stresses the importance of examining the situation, who you are leading, and your personal leadership style when effectively leading others.

Control The management function that assures planned goals and objectives meet the actual activities carried out by a sport business.

Decision Making Choosing between one or more alternatives.

Delegating Giving responsibility to others who are capable of assuming and carrying out responsibilities.

External Environment Environmental trends such as technology, politics, cultural/social factors, competitors, and clientele that a manager must be aware of to manage effectively.

External Focused Departments Departments structure that focuses on the product manufactured, geographic location, or customer serviced.

Fads Temporary marketplace patterns.

Feedback Control Control functions that are executed at the end of a fiscal year, i.e., financial statements, management audits, and performance outcomes.

Internal Environment The various management levels, skills, and roles that managers utilize in day-to-day operations.

Internal Focused Departments Department structure that focuses on the manufacturing process or specific job function involved.

Lead The management skill that enables the sport manager to influence the actions of their subordinates.

Maintenance Factor A component of Herzberg motivation theory that keeps employees satisfied but does not necessarily motivate employees.

Management Information Systems (MIS) Held to compile information needs to assist in daily management functions (planning, organizing, controlling).

Management Science Approach A management theory that utilizes linear programming and forecasting models as a management tool.

Marketing Identifying the needs, wants, and demands of a target audience to assist in an exchange or transaction between the consumer and sport business.

Marketing Management Managing the marketing effort through planning, organizing, and controlling marketing strategies.

Markets Meeting the needs, interests, and demands of target markets.

Minorities Any subgroup of the population that is not male, white, Anglo-Saxon and Protestant.

Mission Statement A statement that clearly defines the primary business goal of the sport enterprise.

Motivate The human behavior trait that causes individuals to exert greater effort toward a given task.

Motivation Goal-directed behavior that can only be inferred, not observed.

Motivation Factor A component of the Herzberg's motivation theory that explains how employees are motivated in the workplace.

Negligence Failure to act as a reasonably prudent person would.

Neoclassical Design Theory Organizational structures that contain low formalization, decentralized authority, and low complexity in design.

Networking The art of communicating with individuals to improve one's work and career status.

Nonprogrammed Decisions Decisions that do not have a set precedence and therefore require group input.

Objectives An important component of the planning process that produces goal-directed behavior in individuals.

Organizational Objectives The end points of the mission statement that specify goals, such as productivity, service, and marketing.

Organizational Strategies Specific avenues for completing organizational objectives.

Organize The management function that defines task and authority relationships for sport business operations.

Plan The management function that establishes specific goals and the activities required to carry out stated goals.

Positioning The concept that stresses the importance of positioning a product, service, or idea in the mind of the consumer.

Power The ability to influence human behavior.

Preliminary Control Control functions that are executed prior to the beginning of a business fiscal year, i.e., hiring, budget development, capital outlay expenditures.

Programmed Decisions Decisions such as policies, rules, and procedures that do not require group input.

Promotions Assists in penetrating target marketings and advertising efforts by utilizing such tools as free samples or discount coupons.

Public Relations Evaluating and monitoring the public opinion of your target publics.

Publicity Nonpaid forms of advertising frequently used by public relations practitioners.

Risk Management A special type of legal crisis planning aimed at preventing legal problems from occurring.

Selective Perception Environmental and personal experiences that cause differences in individual perception.

Societal Marketing A marketing strategy that focuses on product quality and long-run benefit to consumers.

Sport Management The field of study that examines the management of sport consumers, sport participants, and sport spectators.

Sport Violence Emotional or physical behavior with intent to hurt or injure others.

Strategic Planning The long-run vision of an organization typically comprised of a mission statement, organizational objectives, organizational strategy, and a business portfolio. Individual and department plans are derived from the strategic plan.

Systems Approach A management theory that recognizes the importance of how each department in a business functions as a whole.

Tort Liability A legal wrong that results in injury to a person or property.

Trends Established marketplace patterns that help in predicting consumer behavior.

REFERENCES

Chapter 1

Davis, K. "Employee Motivation." *Club Business International,* June 1988, pp. 38–40.

Dubin, R. "Management Meanings, Methods, and Moxie." *Academy of Management Review,* July 1982, pp. 371–379.

McCarthy, J. "Editorial." *Club Business International,* May 1989, p. 2.

McClelland, D. "McClelland: An Advocate of Power" *International Management,* July 1975, pp. 27–29.

Sheffield, E., & Davis, K. "The Scientific Status of Sport Management." *QUEST, 38* (2), 126–134.

Chapter 2

Deveroux, R. "IRSA State of the Industry Report." *IRSA Publications,* June 1991.

Mason, J., Higgins, C., & Williamson, O. J. "Sports Administration Education 15 Years Later." *Athletic Purchasing and Facilities, 5* (1), 44–45.

Rice, L. "Sports Careers Survey" *Sports Careers Publication,* June 1992, p. 46.

Chapter 3

Gemmel, A. "Managing in a Cross-Cultural Environment: The Best of Both Worlds." *Management Solutions,* June 1986, pp. 28–33.

Gribbins, R., & Hunt, S. "Is Management a Science?" *Academy of Management Review,* January 1988, pp. 149–153.

Kast, F., & Rosenzweig, J. "General Systems Theory." *Academy of Management Journal,* December 1972, pp. 447–465.

Kirkland, R. "Entering a New Age of Boundless Competition." *Fortune,* March 14, 1988, p. 42.

Koontz, H. "The Management Theory Jungle Revisited." *Academy of Management Review,* April 1990, pp. 181–195.

Mintzberg, H. "The Managers Job." *Understanding Management.* New York: Harper & Row, 1978, p. 220.

Schoderbek, C., Schoderbek, P., & Kefalas, S. *Management Systems: Conceptual Considerations.* Plano, Texas: Business Publications, 1980.

Stewart, R. "A Model for Understanding Managerial Jobs and Behavior." *Academy of Management Review,* January 1982, pp. 7–13.

Chapter 4

Drucker, P. *The Practice of Management.* New York: Harper & Row, 1954.

Harris, R. "Organizer Plans a No-Frills 1984 Olympics for Los Angeles Amid Strong Objections." *The Wall Street Journal,* January 10, 1983.

Koontz, H. "Making Strategic Planning Work." *Business Horizons,* April 1976, pp. 37–44.

Lawrence, R., & Osborn, R. "Toward an Integrated Theory of Strategy." *Academy of Management Review,* July 1981, pp. 491–498.

MacMillan, I., Hambrick, D., & Day, D. "The Product Portfolio and Profitability—A PIM's Based Analysis of Industrial-Product Businesses." *Academy of Management Journal,* December 1982, pp. 733–755.

Raia, P. *Management by Objectives.* Glenview, IL: Scott, Foresman, 1974.

Roman, M. "The Mission." *Success,* June 1987, pp. 54–57.

Schendel, D., Patton, G., & Riggs, J. "Corporate Turnaround Strategies." *Journal of General Management,* Spring 1976, pp. 3–11.

Simon, H. *The New Science of Management Decision.* New York: Harper & Row, 1960, pp. 5–6.

Chapter 5

Carlyle, R. "Sins of Omission." *Datamation,* 1 January, 1988, pp. 48–54.

Hackman, R., Oldham, G., Janson, R., & Purdy, K. "A New Strategy for Job Enrichment." *California Management Review,* Summer 1975, pp. 57–71.

Hall, C. "The Informal Organizational Chart." *Supervisory Management,* January 1986, p. 41.

Kalzn, S. *Organizing.* New York: McGraw-Hill, 1982.

Keichell, W. "Corporate Strategy for the 1990s." *Fortune,* 29 February, 1988.

McClenahan, J. "Flexible Structures to Absorb the Shocks." *Industry Week,* 18 April, 1988, pp. 41, 44.

Mintzberg, H. *The Structuring of Organizations: A Synthesis of Research.* Englewood Cliffs, NJ: Prentice-Hall, 1979.

Chapter 6

Amend, P. "Input on Output." *Inc.,* April 1985, p. 348.

Arlin, J. "Going the Distance on the Slopes." *The New York Times,* 25 March, 1984.

Augrist, S. "It Pays to Be Patient." *Forbes,* 14 February, 1988, p. 82.

Beach, D. S. *Personnel: The Management of People at Work,* 4th ed. New York: Macmillan, 1980.

Bringham, E. *Fundamentals of Financial Management.* 4th ed. Chicago: Dryden, 1986, p. 644.

Dossett, D., & Greenburg, C. "Goal Setting and Performance Appraisal." *Academy of Management Journal,* December 1981, pp. 767–779.

Eagan, H. *Health Works 1992 Financial Statement.* Cambridge, MA: Porter Square Shopping Center, 1992.

Erickson, D. "Recruitment: Some Unanswered Questions." *Personal Journal,* 1984, p. 136.

Foster, G. *Financial Statement Analysis.* Englewood Cliffs, NJ: Prentice-Hall, 1978.

Knowler, L. *Quality Control by Statistical Methods.* New York: McGraw-Hill, 1969.

Ouchi, W. "The Relationship between Organization Structure and Organizational Control." *Administrative Science Quarterly,* March 1977, pp. 95–113.

Richardson, R. "Managing Your Company's Cash." *Nations Business,* November 1986, pp. 53, 54.

Steinmetz, R., & Todd, L. "Monitoring Day-To-Day Operations-Descretionary Methods." *Journal of General Management,* 32 (2), 1983, pp. 75–89.

Chapter 7

Archer, E. "How to Make a Business Decision: An Analysis of Theory and Practice." *Management Review,* February 1985, pp. 54–61.

Hunsaker, P. "Decision Styles—In Theory and Practice." *Organizational Dynamics,* Autumn 1981, pp. 23–36.

King, J. "Cost-Benefit Analysis for Decision Making." *Journal of Systems Management,* May 1980.

Chapter 8

Berman, P. "New Findings about What Makes Workers Happy." *Working Women,* February 1985, p. 22.

Flamholtz, E. "Personnel Management: The Tenor of Today." *Personnel Management,* June 1987, p. 66.

Herzberg, F. *The Motivation to Work,* 1966. Division of University Microfilms: Books on Demand.

Herzberg, F. "Herzberg on Motivation for the 1990s." *Industry Week,* 1989, pp. 58–63.

Jordan, P. "Effects of an Extrinsic Reward on Intrinsic Motivation: A Field Experiment." *Academy of Management Journal,* June 1986, pp. 405–412.

Maslow, A. *Motivation and Personality,* 2nd ed. New York: Harper & Row, 1970.

McClelland, S. *Motivation in the Workplace.* New York: McGraw-Hill, 1984, pp. 3–8.

McGregor, D. *The Human Side of Enterprise.* New York: McGraw-Hill, 1970.

Schroeder, M. "Watching the Bottom Line Instead of the Clock." *Business Week,* November 7, 1988, p. 136.

Sergiovanni, R. "Motivation: Modifying Maslow's Theory." *Personal Management,* vol. 23, 1980, pp. 23–28.

Sims, H. "Further Thoughts on Punishment in Organizations." *Academy of Management Review,* January 1980, pp. 133–138.

Steers, R., & Porter, L. *Motivation and Work Behavior.* New York: McGraw-Hill, 1982.

Stein, J. "Flexible Benefits." *Houston Post,* August 29, 1982, p. 1BB.

Sussmann, M., & Vecchio, R. P. "A Social Influence Interpretation of Worker Motivation." *Academy of Management Review,* April 1982, pp. 177–186.

Vroom, V. *Work and Motivation.* New York: John Wiley, 1984, pp. 128–129.

Chapter 9

Bacharack, S. B., & Aiken, M. "Communication in Administrative Bureaucracies." *Academy of Management Journal,* March 1987, pp. 365–377.

Blake, R., & Mouton, J. *The Managerial Grid.* Houston, TX: Gulf Publishing, 1964.

Dunham, R. *Organizational Behavior: People and Processes in Management.* Homewood, IL: Richard D. Irwin, 1984.

Goldhaber, G. *Organizational Communication,* 3rd ed. Dubuque, IA: Wm. C. Brown, 1983.

Hall, J. "Put Communication Theory into Practice." *American Business Communication Association Bulletin, 36* (1), 1973, pp. 6–8.

House, P. "Path-Goal Theory of Leadership." *Journal of Contemporary Business,* Autumn 1984, pp. 81–97.

Likert, R. *New Patterns of Management.* New York: McGraw-Hill, 1961.

Putnam, L., & Pacanowsky, M. *Communication and Organization: An Interpretive Approach.* Beverly Hills, CA: Sage Publications, 1983.

Stogdill, R. "Personal Factors Associated with Leadership." *Journal of Applied Psychology,* January 1948, pp. 35–71.

Tannenbaum, R., & Schmidt, W. "How to Choose a Leadership Pattern." *Harvard Business Review,* May–June 1973, pp. 162–180.

Chapter 10

Boyatzis, R. *The Competent Manager: A Model for Effective Performance.* New York: John Wiley & Sons, 1982.

Davis, T. "Leadership Reexamined: A Behavioral Approach." *Academy of Management Review,* April 1979, pp. 237–248.

Hatakeyama, Y. "The Unsung Hero of Japanese Management: The Middle Manager." *Management Review,* April 1989, p. 33.

McClelland, D., & Boyatzis, R. "Leadership Motive Pattern and Long-Term Success in Management." *Journal of Applied Psychology,* December 1982, pp. 737–743.

Mintzberg, H. *The Nature of Managerial Work.* Englewood Cliffs, NJ: Prentice-Hall, 1980.

Rodgers, B. *Getting the Best Out of Yourself and Others.* New York: Harper & Row, 1988.

Chapter 11

Blake, G., & Bly, R. *How to Promote Your Own Business.* New York: New American Library, 1983, pp. 56–59.

Childs, K. "Attitude Roots." *Advertising Age,* January 1980, pp. 31–35.

Cutlip, S., Center, A., & Broom, G. *Effective Public Relations.* Englewood Cliffs, NJ: Prentice-Hall, 1985, pp. 3–6.

Frank, R., Massy, W., & Wind, Y. *Market Segmentation.* Englewood Cliffs, NJ: Prentice-Hall, 1972, pp. 27–31.

Harlow, R. "Building a Public Relations Definition." *Public Relations Review,* (2), Winter 1976, p. 36.

Kotler, P. *Principles of Marketing,* 2nd ed. Englewood Cliffs, NJ: Prentice-Hall, 1983, pp. 6–13.

Lindenmann, W. "Hunches No Longer Suffice." *Public Relations Journal,* Vol. 36, June 1980, pp. 9–13.

Naisbitt, J. *Megatrends, Ten New Directions Transforming Our Lives.* New York: Warner Books, 1982, p. 12.

Paisley, W. "Public Communication Campaigns, the American Experience." *Public Communication Campaigns.* Beverly Hills: Sage Publications, 1981, pp. 15–21.

Reis, A., & Trout, J. *Positioning: The Battle for Your Mind.* New York: McGraw-Hill, 1986, pp. 5–10.

Rossi, P., & Freeman, H. *Evaluation: A Systematic Approach,* 2nd ed. Beverly Hills, CA: Sage Publications, 1982, p. 27.

Chapter 12

Allison, K. *Sports Leagues and the Antitrust Laws, Government, and The Sports Business.* R. Noll, Ed. New York: Macmillan, 1974, pp. 46–55.

Cardozo, B. *The Nature of the Judicial Process.* New Haven and London: Yale University Press, 1962, pp. 18–19.

Holmes, H. *"The Path of the Law." 10 Harvard Law Review,* 1920, pp. 167–169.

Pound, R. "Common Law and Legislation." *21 Harvard Law Review,* 1908, pp. 383, 385.

Prosser, W. *Law of Torts.* St. Paul, MN: West Publishing Co., 1974, pp. 3–6.

Prosser, W., Wade, J., & Schwartz, V. *Torts, Cases and Materials,* 6th ed. Mineola, NY: Foundation Press, 1976, pp. 45–51.

Terry, R. "Negligence." *29 Harvard Law Review,* (40), 1915, pp. 291–293.

Wong, G. *The Law of Amateur Sports.* St. Paul, MN: West Publishing Co., 1988, pp. 298–305.

Chapter 13

Bralove, M. "Direct Data: Some Chief Executives Bypass and Irk Staffs in Getting Information." *The Wall Street Journal,* January 12, 1983.

Bulkeley, W. "Microcomputers Gaining Primacy, Forcing Changes in the Industry." *The Wall Street Journal,* January 13, 1983.

Department of Commerce. *U.S. Industrial Outlook 1988—Electronic Components.* Washington, DC: Government Printing Office, 1988.

Dressang, J. "High-Tech System Lets Firms Publish." *USA Today,* January 16, 1987, p. 1Bff.

Dykeman, J. "Optical Disk: A Technology on the Move." *Modern Office Technology,* June 1988, p. 83.

Elmer-Dewitt, P. "The Next Major Battleground." *Time,* April 25, 1988, p. 83.

Gannes, Stuart. "Computer Quake." *Fortune Magazine,* August 1, 1988, p. 43.

Oeftering, A. "Everyone's a Publisher." *Management World,* February–March, 1987, pp. 42–43.

Robinson, A. "One Billion Transistors on a Chip?" *Science,* January 20, 1983, p. 267ff.

Chapter 14

Brubaker, B. "U.S. Sports Are Pushed to the Edge." *The Chicago Tribune,* August 5, 1990, p. C3.

Carpenter, L., & Acosta, V. *Women in Intercollegiate Sport.* Brooklyn, NY: Brooklyn College, 1990.

Donnell, S., & Hall, J. "Men and Women as Managers: A Significant Case of No Significant Difference." *Organizational Dynamics,* Spring 1980.

Kotler, P. *Principles of Marketing.* Englewood Cliffs, NJ: Prentice-Hall, 1983, pp. 608–615.

Lapchick, R. "The Promised Land." *Fractured Focus.* Lexington, MA: Lexington Books, 1986.

Managed Recreation Research Report. *Recreation and Leisure Management.* 1988, pp. 13–15.

Newsome, M. "Drug Free." *USOC Drug Education Handbook 1989–92.* Colorado Springs, CO: USOC, pp. 21–44.

Chapter 15

Bialkowski, D. "Launching a New Club—Denver Club Defies the Odds in Depressed Market." *Club Industry,* April 1991, pp. 22–24.

Hildreth, S. "The Superachievers: What It Takes to Become a Top Five Club." *Club Business International,* June 1991, pp. 16–25.

Chapter 16

Mattson, R. "The New Boston Garden." *Informational Package.* Delaware Corporation, October 22, 1992.

Mayo, M. "Is It the Place or the Show?" *Miami Sun-Sentinel,* September 20, 1992, pp. 1c, 7c.

Mon, G. Interview: Joe Robbie Stadium, November 4, 1992.

Sauers, M. *Spectacor Corporation Informational Package,* 1992.

Chapter 17

American Marketing Association. Conference Keynote Address, New Orleans, LA, March 1991.

Bulkeley, W. "Reebok Posts 39% Rise in Earnings." *Wall Street Journal,* July 23, 1991, p. A5.

Grim, Matthew. *Adweeks Marketing Week,* Vol. 32, Jan. 24, 1990, p. 34.

Haves, M. "Nike Approach to Women." *New York Times,* March 29, 1991, p. D5.

Kerwin, K. "Reebok Pump on Top." *Business Week,* June 19, 1991, p. 54.

McCoy, C. "Nike Comfortable with Estimates. *Wall Street Journal,* July 10, 1991, p. A7.

McNerney, J. "The Athletic Shoe Industry—The Power of the Consumer." *New York Times,* Sept. 30, 1990, p. 12S.

Moody's Industrial Manual. 1991, p. 5848.

Pererira, J. "Athletic Shoe Sales Are Expected to Be Sluggish in the U.S." *Wall Street Journal,* April 1, 1991, p. C6.

Sauers, M. *Spectacor Corporation Informational Package,* 1992.

SEC Data Base. CDRom, Snell Library, Northeastern University, Boston, MA, 1991.

Wall Street Journal. "Digest of Earnings Report." July 23, 1991, p. A14.

CREDITS

INDEX

Page numbers that are *italicized* refer to illustrations. An *f, t,* or *p,* before a page number refers to a figure (*f*), or table (*t*), or picture (*p*) on that page.